Contents

LESBIAN RELATIONSHIPS

The Essential Guide

Nicci Talbot

Contains adult content

Lesbian Relationships: The Essential Guide is also available in accessible formats for people with any degree of visual impairment. The large print edition and e-book (with accessibility features enabled) are available from Need2Know. Please let us know if there are any special features you require and we will do our best to accommodate your needs.

First published in Great Britain in 2013 by
Need2Know
Remus House
Coltsfoot Drive
Peterborough
PE2 9BF
Telephone 01733 898103
Fax 01733 313524
www.need2knowbooks.co.uk

Introduction

According to National Statistics, there are around three million lesbian and bisexual women in the UK, an estimated 5-7% of the population. Studies indicate that female sexuality – the idea that our orientation is less fixed than we thought – is more common in women than in men, says Bonnie Zylbergold, assistant editor of *American Sexuality*. A recent article in *Oprah* magazine points to a rise in expansive vocabulary to describe sexuality: 'transgender, transsexual, transvestite, boi, heteroflexible, intersex, gender queer'.

Many women who love women do not identify as bisexual or lesbian, given that the labels are quite loaded in terms of looks, attitude and political stance. *'I am single right now. I've had one long-term relationship with a man, one long-term relationship with a woman, equal numbers of male and female sexual partners, more short-term relationships with men and only men in the last four years. I dislike labels so don't identify as "bisexual".'* (Jane, 43).

More celebrities are openly out in the media – boxer Nicola Adams topped the *Independent on Sunday Pink List* in 2012, Clare Balding was also in the limelight with a new book out, and Mary Portas was revamping the British high street as Queen of Shops.

Binnie Klein, a Connecticut-based psychotherapist and lecturer at Yale's Department of Psychiatry believes alternative relationships are on the rise. 'It's clear that a change in sexual orientation is imaginable to more people than ever before, and there's more opportunity – and acceptance – to cross over the line,' she says, adding that six of her married female patients in the past few years have fallen in love with women.

Feminist philosopher Susan Bordo, PhD, a professor of English, Gender and Women's Studies at the University of Kentucky, says that in the current environment, more women are stepping out of the conventional gender box. 'When a taboo is lifted or diminished, it's going to leave people freer to pursue things.' However, she also points out that we still have judgements and opinions around what's acceptable for lesbians. 'Just look at the cast of the L-Word and it's clear that only a certain kind of lesbian – slim and elegant or butch in just the right androgynous way – is acceptable to mainstream culture.'

There are lesbians who come out in their teens and those who have had heterosexual relationships and a family, choosing to have a relationship with a woman in their 30s or 40s.

Whether you've just come out as a lesbian or are in a relationship with a woman for the first time in your 40s, this book includes information, resources and advice to help you make the most of your sex life, community, relationships and family.

I had a few requests for information on how to meet more women so chapter 4 explores dating in all its guises – where to find women if you don't want to be part of the scene. While the gay scene is vibrant and well developed in cities such as Manchester, London, Bristol and Brighton, it's less 'in your face' in smaller towns like mine. In Hastings, there's an active LGBT (lesbian, gay, bisexual and transgender) community but you need to subscribe to mailing lists to find out what's going on. I interviewed several local lesbian and bisexual women and found that many older women (30s and 40s+) were not interested in being part of the scene:

'I dipped a toe in the scene but found it very based on image. I'm too fat and old to fit into that and not nearly shallow enough. At my age, it's hard to meet anyone who's still single, male or female, but at the moment I'm concentrating on my career and hoping that one day, I'll meet the right person for me, be they male or female, black, white, Asian or whatever. If it doesn't happen, it doesn't happen. I won't consider my life a failure.' (Ruth, 36).

'I moved to a rural area a year ago but have met some nice lesbians and new friends through a lesbian walking group. I feel I'm too old for the scene! I was much more involved in my early 20s when I lived in a big city. That said, having lesbian friends and social contact is very important to me. I value knowing other lesbian couples and being able to confide in friends about relationship issues. My partner and I will travel to attend special events such as BDSM dyke play parties. I think a useful concept to explore is keeping the sex and sexuality part of your relationship alive when you become "best friends". This hasn't

happened with us, but I know others for whom the relationship is primarily a friendship and sexuality is smothered/stagnates/doesn't feature anymore.'
(Anna, 39)

Other women echoed this viewpoint so I have included chapters on sex and desire, intimacy, foreplay, fantasy and masturbation. The charming term 'lesbian bed death' is prolific, which seems a bit depressing and puts me in mind of a road sign with a double bed crossed through. Sexologist Pepper Schwartz coined the term in 1983 after she found that lesbians in long-term relationships reported less sexual intimacy than gay men or heterosexual couples. Still, it doesn't mean it's a foregone conclusion. I found experts who challenge this presumption. Sexual pleasure is pretty important to most of us, and sex and physical intimacy is what differentiates a partnership from a friendship so we'll look at ways to keep it on the agenda.

Female sexuality is constantly evolving and there have been changes in attitudes and awareness since 1983. We have sex manuals, DVDs and erotica, new products and sex toys, and more scientific research in progress showing what happens in the body and brain when we orgasm. In other words, we have a choice about our sex lives and libido and we don't have to accept the status quo.

Part of the reason such myths pervade is that not enough lesbians and bisexual women talk about their sex lives. Researchers at The Center For Sexual Health Promotion at Indiana University collected data for a contemporary survey of lesbian relationships* and found a much lower response rate amongst lesbian and bisexual women than for heterosexual couples in similar surveys. I had a similar experience with my online survey in that many of the sex questions were left unanswered, even though responses could be anonymous.

The editor of *DIVA* magazine, the UK's leading lesbian magazine, asked me to share any results for lesbians in a libido survey I ran last year, so it's a topic of interest. Researchers only have our survey responses to go on so if you want to see improvements to sexual healthcare for lesbians fill in an academic-led

---

* *National Survey of Sexual Health & Behaviour (NSSHB) by The Center For Sexual Health Promotion at Indiana University.* Reece, M., Herbenick, D., Schick, V., Sanders, S. A., Dodge, B. and Fortenberry, J. D. (2010), Background and Considerations on the National Survey of Sexual Health and Behavior (NSSHB) from the Investigators. Journal of Sexual Medicine, 7: 243–245. doi: 10.1111/j.1743-6109.2010.02038.

sex survey if you get the opportunity. That way we have a better chance of getting accurate and useful information out there which reflects lesbians today rather than relying on data cobbled together from heterosexual surveys.

20th century lesbian life may be more visible than in the past says Rebecca Jennings, author of *A Lesbian History of Britain: Love & Sex Between Women Since 1500*, but it's no less complicated. Civil partnerships are accepted in Scotland and the UK and medical advances mean that two women can now raise a family together. However, Jennings points out that there is a lack of oral histories. We need more shared experiences from women who share their lives with other women, as not much has been documented over the years.

My local library has an oral history project for the LGBT community and is recruiting volunteers to interview local people. It's an opportunity to share your life story and participate in other people's, a rewarding project that will expand your connections and create a sense of place and community. If that appeals to you why not contact your local library and see if they will do something similar? I would love to read your oral histories, anonymous or named. Send them to nicci@rudemagazine.co.uk and I'll publish them on a website to accompany this book.

Another way to expand on this is to get a local women's group going. Between 1890 and 1930 the American heiress Natalie Clifford Barney set up a weekly Salon in Paris to discuss lesbian topics and eroticism. She was inspired to update the idea of 'Lesbos' and wanted to discuss issues relevant to women at the time. This seems like a tradition worth maintaining. As feminist writer Naomi McCormick points out, emotional, mental and ideological connections between women are just as important as a genital and sexual connection. We need both for a satisfying relationship.

Chapter One

Coming Out

Coming out is a lifelong process, whether you're lesbian, gay or bisexual. It doesn't matter if you are in your teens and thinking about the best way to tell your mum, or in a new relationship with a woman in your 40s – post marriage and with kids. A quarter of all calls to the Lesbian & Gay Foundation Helpline are about coming out and the best way to deal with it.

Studies have found that female sexuality is more fluid than we think and a woman may be attracted to both men and women at different stages of her life. Bisexuality isn't a trendy choice, as the media perceives it to be. It can sometimes be more difficult to come out to friends and family because they already have judgements around your sexuality based on the relationships you've had previously. You may face hostility from lesbian friends who think you're 'sitting on the fence'. Coming out as bisexual is harder in some ways because things aren't so black and white. You may have several relationships over your lifetime with men and women and choose not to be monogamous. Your lifestyle choices may be a challenge for people to come to terms with.

I did an online survey of lesbian and bi women for this book and one of the questions was about coming out and why it's important to do it. Most felt that it's a must to be able to live your life honestly and freely. It will free you up psychologically and energetically to get out there, meet new people and have new experiences. 'Making the decision to share your sexuality also challenges you to think about and acknowledge it', says the Terence Higgins Trust (THT). 'The first thing you should think about is whether you accept your sexuality; do you feel confident enough to talk about it with others?'

'Coming out is a lifelong process, whether you're lesbian, gay or bisexual.'

A historical context

'The historical contexts of "coming out" (of the closet) are within the framework of emancipation, identity and protest. From its early conceptualisation of being a single, monolithic event, it is now considered as a process of development and identity formation. Models describing the processes have been reported, but these have come under heavy criticism over the years for their linear paradigm, their "one-size fits all" approach (not taking into account Queer sexualities other than gay or lesbian, and not being culture-sensitive), and the suggestion of sexuality being an immutable phenomenon.

It is a contentious issue particularly for the British, Minority, Ethnic (BME) population, where white British culture, identity and behaviour isn't applicable.'

Source: Coming Out, Staying In, and Stepping In and Out of the Closet: Questions of Black and Minority Ethnic-Queer Identities, Roshan das Nair, Department of Clinical and Neuropsychology, Queens Medical Centre, Nottingham.

What is 'coming out'?

In his book *Pink Therapy: A Guide For Counsellors & Therapists Working With LGBT Clients* (Open University Press, 1996), Dominic Davies describes 'coming out' as 'a phenomenon [which] has been identified as a crucial part of the development of lesbian and gay identity'. This chapter is dedicated to the process and explores three of the established psychological models and their flaws in relation to people of colour, disability and bisexuality.

'Coming out involves a complex process of intra and interpersonal transformation, often beginning in adolescence and extending well into adulthood which lead to, accompany and follow the events associated with acknowledgment of one's sexual orientation,' say psychologists Hanley and Hackenbruck. Davies also quotes Cohen and Stein: '[it] refers to a complicated developmental process which involves, at a psychological level, a person's awareness and acknowledgment of homosexual thoughts and feelings for some persons. "Coming out" leads to public identification as a gay man or lesbian. Various factors will affect the relative positive or negative meanings the individual places on the identity which emerges as a result of the coming out process.'

Why is it important?

Psychoanalyst E H Erikson (1946) believes that individuals need to accomplish several developmental tasks as part of our identity development and wellbeing. This includes the integration of our sexuality. Because societal norms are largely anti-gay then developmental tasks need to include dealing with homophobia. Davies points out that a number of psychological models of 'coming out' have been developed over the past 20 years and explores three of them: Cass Model, Coleman Model and Woodman-Lenna Model. He says that one of the difficulties with the models is that they presume a person is either heterosexual or gay – sexuality is not black and white and sexual orientation can change over time.

The Models

- Cass Model (1979) identifies six stages of coming out – identity confusion, identity comparison, identity tolerance, identity acceptance, identity pride and identity synthesis.

- Coleman Model (1981/2) – a five-stage model – pre-coming out, coming out, exploration, first relationships and identity integration.

- Woodman-Lenna Model (1980) – a four-stage model – denial, identity confusion, bargaining and depression.

Davies says that despite their flaws the models are useful in that they give an indication of where a person is now in their experiences and observations. We need to be aware that our development isn't linear and that we can experience several stages simultaneously. Coming out is related to the development of personal and social identity, self-esteem and authentic, satisfying relationships with others.

'The process of coming out is also heavily influenced by a number of significant variables: gender, race or ethnic group, locale (urban Vs rural), the extent of sexual variation, the values and attitudes of society at the time, individual variation (including the individual's own psychological make up), family circumstances etc., and physical ability or sensory impairment,' says Davies.

Counselling – an initial step

Charlotte Powolny is a counsellor and psychotherapist based in East Sussex. She explains some of the potential issues around coming out and how to deal with the emotional aspects:

'One particular client who sought counselling had some issues with their sexuality when things changed with a female friend. Boundaries were crossed and this left the person confused and struggling with their religion, which added to the roller coaster of emotions. Because of religion this person was unable to talk to friends or family so carried this around with them for a number of years resulting in depression.

'The feelings experienced by this person were rejection, shame, denial, confusion, repression of feelings and struggling with religious beliefs.

'By talking about the different stages of coming out the client began to accept their sexual orientation and developed a sense of contentment with being a lesbian.

'The first person they shared their story with was a counsellor because it was somebody they did not know and they did not want to be judged by significant others. Disclosure was a slow process for this person.

'This client told me that they made a brave choice about coming out but stated they are the happiest they have ever been in their life. They are currently in a lesbian relationship where both families and friends are very accepting of their relationship despite religious beliefs.

'Coming out is experienced differently by each individual from all walks of life, age, background and minority groups.

'Talking about it to friends, family, significant others, support groups and researching on the Internet are the first steps to acceptance whilst gaining insight and an understanding about a person's sexual orientation.

'When you come to identify your sexuality, have accepted it, and have decided to come out of the closet, you may want to stop and think about whether you are doing the right thing by confiding in certain people at this point. The key is to know if you are ready, then choose the first people you tell for their potential as positive supporters, and then decide whether or not you would like some of your more casual acquaintances to know.

'Have patience – Remember that it took time to get used to your sexuality, so others may need time to get used to the idea too. Last of all be proud of who you are!'

Who to tell first

As Powolny says, sometimes it can be helpful to talk things through with a counsellor first so you are clear on your own feelings and feel ready to talk to others. Think about whom in your life will be the most supportive and tell them first. Talk in private if you can and when you are not stressed or rushing around. Be prepared for common reactions (see overleaf) and think about your responses – an instinctive reaction from family may be fear-based around what others will think or the possibility of not having any grandchildren. In this scenario, explain that it is still possible for you to become a parent if you want to be. Give your parents time to come to terms with things and they will most likely support you in the long run.

'If you come out to your parents and they react badly, they can get support from groups around the country that are run by parents of lesbians and gay men. They will be able to offer your parents support and information on coming to terms with your sexuality', says THT. See the links on their website (www.tht.org.uk) to FFLAG (Friends and Family of Lesbians and Gays).

'Sometimes it can be helpful to talk things through with a counsellor first so you are clear on your own feelings and feel ready to talk to others.'

Common reactions

LGBT Youth Scotland ran a national project called Green Light (www.lgbtyouth. org.uk) to support LGBT people in coming out. They suggest preparing a response to the following common reactions from friends and family:

- How do you know? Are you sure?
- What does lesbian or bisexual mean?
- Does it mean you'll never have kids?
- It's a difficult life to lead.
- Don't tell anyone (how will you react if triggered by such a comment if your mum or dad are ashamed of your sexuality and fear ridicule?)
- It's against our religion . . .
- I don't want to know you anymore.
- It's just a phase.
- I feel like I don't know you anymore.
- You don't look gay . . .
- How do people have sex with someone of the same gender?

Coming out on the scene

'Decide whether you want to join the local gay scene – pubs, clubs, newsletters, etc. are a great way of building confidence and meeting new people in a similar situation.'

Decide whether you want to join the local gay scene – pubs, clubs, newsletters, etc. are a great way of building confidence and meeting new people in a similar situation. Feeling part of a community is important for self-esteem and personal development. Most towns have a LGBT group and there are youth groups for younger lesbians. You can talk to others in the same situation and be referred for counselling if you need support.

Here are your stories on coming out as a lifelong process:

'I came out to some friends when I had met my partner but before we started dating. She is my only sexual relationship. Some friends I came out to after I had started dating my wife, and most friends were happy for me. Others had an issue with who I was dating and tried very hard to split us up. We are no longer

friends. My family weren't as accepting. My sister and brothers were fine with it but my mother hated it and made that quite clear. She spent three years trying to split us up before I finally cut her out of my life for good. My grandparents were fine with it and very accepting of my partner. Other family members were vocal about it being unnatural. It was a difficult three years but once I'd stopped listening to them and only spoke to those who were happy for me, my life became a lot better. Coming out is definitely a lifelong process. I don't look like your stereotypical lesbian so everyone assumes I'm married to a man. I tell some people straight away, others not at all and some when they ask about my husband – I tell them about my wife!' (Anon, 30, Midlands).

'I came out when I left my husband. That was about four years ago. Some members of the family accepted it, others proved how homophobic they are. I now only positively communicate with half of my family. Coming out is a lifelong process and it is annoying that it has to be. But equally it's empowering too. At work I am continually being outed or outing myself (I work with 16-19 year-olds as a college tutor). I feel that it is a good thing in this respect as students seek me for advice and guidance and have a positive role model. I like to be able to talk freely about my family life (I have children). I am not the only lesbian member of staff either – just glancing around the room there are six lezzers and one bisexual.' (JB, 37, Leeds).

'My family don't know, but that's only because we don't discuss things like that. They just don't seem to be interested in my romantic relationships (maybe it's embarrassing for them?) but that's fine with me. Most of my friends know and I always tell my partners.' (Alice, 36, Kent).

'18 years old. Scared, ashamed, excited and different. Yes, coming out is a lifelong process. I have to come out every time I develop a new relationship both socially and, where appropriate, professionally.' (Caroline, 44, London).

'When I was 19 and I moved away from home (Liverpool) to university. I'm not close to my family and it didn't make much difference – although my auntie (who brought me up instead of my mother) refused to let me feed the dog that night. It brought me closer to my mum for a while, oddly, as she wasn't phased by it at all. Then a year later she used it against me in an argument with my auntie, blaming her for how I turned out, and I didn't see her for two years. Since then it's never been discussed. I tend not to see coming out as a process. I'm a lesbian and that's how I live my life. I have never made a big deal out of telling *anyone, it's just a fact and I discuss my life and girlfriend/wife as a matter of fact, the same way straight people do. Due to things I've done with my time, I usually refer to LGBT groups in any job interviews, so my being gay is a fact up front, and I've never had to think about when/if to make a point of telling people.'* (Jo, 40, Hastings).

'I came out as a lesbian at 19, but decided six months later that I'd only done so because of the pressure to be "one or the other" in the lesbian community. I stopped using any label to identify sexually a few years ago and describe myself as "sexual". Coming out is what I choose it to be, it's only difficult if the opinion of those I'm discussing my sexuality and sexual life with matters. For the most part the opinion others have of me doesn't matter, so it's not an issue anymore.' (Beth, 43, Preston).

'In 1999. Those I thought would be great weren't. Those I thought would be troubled were great. Lifelong process, yes . . . but in the past decade or so it's got easier as it's more accepted.' (DK, 45, Derbyshire).

'I came out in Year 11 of secondary school. Many didn't seem surprised. I was relieved that people knew and I didn't have to hide anything. It's something that must be done if you are to be happy with your life.' (Zoe, 20, Lincolnshire).

'I came out first of all to friends and a teacher when I was about 14/15. Their responses were fine, I was sharing with them what I believed my orientation to be but nothing else about me changed. At 16 I had my first girlfriend – she said she was bi and didn't want her family to know. I came out to my mum at 16 after starting a 6th form college where I met and became part of a group of lesbian friends. My mum was very upset and didn't speak to me for a while. I thought I was going to have to leave home. We moved a year later and I was separated from my friends. I struggled to meet new lesbians. The only other one at college was a born-again Christian and wanted to convert me to Christianity and a straight life. I wanted to convince her it was okay to be gay. We didn't get past stalemate.

'I was still living at home and ended up going out with a guy 13 years senior. I told him I was a lesbian and he said it didn't matter to him. I lost my virginity to him and we went out for a year. As soon as I was able I left home for university and left my "boyfriend". Once living in a city again I soon found a group of lesbian friends. I was always out as a lesbian: in college and university.

'I came out to my dad when I was in my early 20s and he was fine about it. The rest of the family were fine and just wanted me to be happy. My mum tolerated it and allowed me to bring girlfriends home for Christmas. When it came to our civil partnership, she initially said she wouldn't come, but she did and as the ceremony ended, she finally understood and accepted the validity of my relationship. She loves my partner like another daughter.

'Each time I start a new job (I do mainly short-term contracts) I have to come out all over again. I mention my partner and try to get her gender into the conversation early so there is no confusion. I don't think I look particularly straight, but people tend to presume I am unless I state otherwise. The assumptions can be wearing. I am out to everyone I know, the only exceptions are clients I have worked with in my capacity as a health/social care professional or research participants in my capacity as a researcher. I don't keep it a secret but I do like my personal life to be boundaried and see no reason why I should tell these people anything about my relationships. That said, I would never deny my sexuality if someone asked outright.' (Anna, 39, Devon).

'At 15 – I was forced to come out to my family by my girlfriend at the time. My friends were fine apart from two who spread it around school and I was bullied – had stuff thrown at me including a log, milkshake and hot dog. It sounds funny but in reality it was cruel and miserable. I had bad reactions from my family and felt awful about it. They banned my girlfriend from the house and I had to see her secretly for the remaining year of our relationship – quite a feat when I couldn't drive and live in the middle of nowhere! I wasn't near mature enough to handle the emotions of coming out. I agree about the lifelong process – it took my family time to get used to the idea of my being gay.' (Kadie, 21).

'The first process is coming out to yourself: 16, then family: 24-28 (not all at once). The reaction was overwhelmingly positive – also from work mates. People really don't care anymore. What has been interesting is that family then have their own 'coming out' – for example my mum, and being asked when I would marry and have children.' (Rachel, 40, Brighton).

'I came out when I was 40 and left my husband for another woman (not the one I am with now). His family were horrified. My friends and family were very understanding and supportive. My two children were surprised but have *adapted amazingly. I still never know when to come out to new work colleagues – do I need to? I am a nurse and I never come out to patients, why would I?'* (Justine, 42, Middlesex).

Summing up

- Coming out is a lifelong process whether you're in your teens or 30s/40s. It can be more complicated if you are bisexual because you're often seen to be 'sitting on the fence' or 'having the best of both worlds' as if your sexuality is a choice. You're attracted to both men and women and often it's about the person rather than the gender. Research has shown that female sexuality is a lot more fluid than we think.

- Most women say that despite it being difficult in some cases (parents, most notably) having that conversation is worth it. Being honest and owning your sexuality is empowering and enables you to live freely and fully. It brings new energy, opportunities and people into your life.

- You may find it helpful to talk to a counsellor first who has an independent and professional view. When you are ready, talk to someone you trust who you know will be positive and a source of support for you. This will make it easier to talk to family and those you know who may find it more difficult to come to terms with. Give people time to take it on board and be prepared for common questions. It may have taken you time to come to terms with conflicting feelings over your sexuality and it can be the same process for those you are close to.

Chapter Two

Sex and Desire

There are some common myths around lesbian relationships and female sexuality:

* 'Lesbian bed death' – a term coined by sexologist Pepper Schwartz in 1996 after she found that lesbian couples have less sex in long-term relationships than gay men and heterosexual couples.

* Female relationships are less sexually focused and have more emphasis on emotional support and friendship.

* Lesbian relationships are short-lived and intense, they move quickly and don't last (I came across a widely held view that lesbian relationships struggle beyond that two-year mark and that old joke: what does a lesbian woman bring on her second date? Her suitcase . . .

* Passion and stability aren't compatible.

* I want more sex than my partner.

* I want less sex as I get older.

Anna Samson is a lesbian, 39, who writes a blog about female sexuality, www. theladygarden.com. She responded to my online survey about sex and relationships between women and said the following: 'My partner and I will travel to attend special events such as BDSM dyke play parties. I think a useful concept to explore is keeping the sex and sexuality part of your relationship alive when you become "best friends". This hasn't happened with us, but I know others for whom the relationship is primarily a friendship and sexuality is smothered/stagnates/just doesn't feature anymore.'

'In a previous long-term relationship (six years) we only had sex for the first two, which was frustrating, as once we hit a certain point it was impossible to contemplate ever doing anything rude together again. This did eventually contribute to our break up.' (Jo, 40, Hastings).

So what can you do if you're in this situation, you still love your partner and feel a strong emotional connection but the passion has gone?

Your sexual history

It's helpful to do this exercise on your own and with a partner when you're ready. Write down your sexual history, what went well, what didn't and what you've learned from your relationships. Have you had a gap between relationships to process things and get to know yourself a little bit better? Next, write down how important sex and physical intimacy is to you and how you show this (masturbation, compliments to partner, things you buy, etc.). What was your sex life like in the beginning when you were first attracted to one another? What was the spark that set it apart from other close female friendships and made you become lovers? Can you track any changes or triggers over the past year that have led to a lack of sex and intimacy?

Diary dates

Get your diary out and see how much of a priority your sex life is. Are there play dates or shopping dates in there for the next few weeks ahead? Do you have things to look forward to together? Is there time set aside to relax and do nothing together (which will often lead to sex and intimacy if you remove it from the domestic)? A friend of mine is dating a new lady and they have set dates in the diary for the next six months ahead. She said the other day that work and other things feel so easy because she feels supported in an emotional sense. She is more relaxed and therefore able to switch gear into physical intimacy that much quicker. Her partner is the first to actively schedule time together and rather than being something that's not spontaneous it has given her a sense of security and anticipation.

24-hour foreplay

Dr Glenda Corwin is a clinical psychologist specialising in sexual intimacy issues for women in same-sex relationships. In her book *Sexual Intimacy for Women: A Guide for Same-Sex Couples*, she introduces the concept of 24-hour foreplay as a way to keep your sexuality alive in long-term relationships. In 2007, she conducted an online survey into sexual patterns in female-to-female relationships and 90% of respondents said they thought regular sex was important in a primary relationship; that it could bring you closer and forge a deeper connection. Even those who weren't having regular sex said it was important to them. What struck Corwin is that the women who weren't sexually active with partners never planned time for intimacy, seeing it as 'contrived'. 'Such high value is placed on sexual intimacy, but apparently, so little is done to nurture it,' she says.

Corwin says she knows it's possible to keep sexual passion alive. In her clinical experience, she has found that around 20% of lesbian couples who live together meet the criteria of being what therapists refer to as 'sexually active' (SA) – they have sexual contact two or more times a month. She says: 'These SA women are very intentional about their sexual relationships, protecting their privacy and time for intimate focus on each other. They take responsibility for their own sexuality, consciously engaging in thoughts and activities that make them feel more sexual. They also pay attention to how they can support or sabotage each other in the sexual area, and they work as a team to create conditions that are conducive to sexual intimacy.'

So how to do this? She suggests keeping an erotic diary and tracking your sexual thoughts throughout the day, noticing what turns you on or off at different times of the month. Find ways to self-stimulate through erotica, fantasy and sensual experiences such as massage and yoga. Find activities that make you feel alive and passionate. Schedule in solo pleasure sessions and generally pay as much attention to your intimate life and connection with self as you do other facets of life – your career and friendships. I take little play breaks when I'm writing and find I'm more energised and relaxed following an orgasm so it's easier to write and come up with ideas. I'm more open to opportunities, more present in my body and seem to connect better with others. It's important to give yourself that time to nurture your body and libido.

What is sexual desire?

Sexuality studies indicate that 43% of women have some difficulty with sexuality, be it lack of desire, orgasm problems or painful sex. We can look at desire as a physical urge for sex and orgasm and an emotional urge for closeness and intimacy with ourselves and a partner. For most women the latter is just as important. Desire feeds desire so it's about feeling wanted too – it boosts our self-esteem, sexual identity and confidence. Regular sex and orgasms make us want more too – it's cyclic and our bodies get used to a certain level of sexual activity and feeling good.

Types of desire

Sex therapists define different types of desire, which is helpful as you can see that much of your sex drive and libido is under your conscious control – it's not something outside of you and needs to be nurtured. Here's a brief overview of the different types of desire so you can see the process of falling in lust/love and how it changes in a long-term relationship.

Spontaneous desire

'Limerance' is a state of intoxication when you can't think of anything else but your lover. The name is attributed to psychologist Dorothy Tennov and defined as 'an involuntary cognitive and emotional state, with continuous, intrusive thoughts and intense longing for the other'. It is a romantic phase but a temporary one and characterised by high sexual activity. Neurochemistry levels in the brain change – dopamine, serotonin and norepinephrine – which can make sex feel exciting. It also creates a sense of anxiety (will it last?) leaving us with a roller coaster of emotions. When we have sex it increases testosterone production, which makes us crave more sex, and orgasms produce oxytocin in the brain, which bond us to our partner. Women release more oxytocin than men so we have a strong need for an emotional connection as well as a physical one. Bring two women together and this need is intensified, hence the pattern of high levels of physical activity at the start of a same-sex relationship.

'Sexuality studies indicate that 43% of women have some difficulty with sexuality be it lack of desire, orgasm problems or painful sex.'

Studies show that this state of being can last anything from a few months to two years. It has to evolve otherwise we'd get nothing done. Corwin points out that although it's predicable and temporary it's still a positive thing because it shows you what's possible in your relationship. If you know the factors involved in sexual excitement you can recreate them (the situation or circumstance) later on in your relationship. She means that sexual desire is a choice and intent, and not something that's outside of your control and subject to inevitable decline. I find this idea empowering as it means you can take charge of your sexuality and sex life.

Think back to when you had a hot date or first met your lover, she says, and you'll see how much planning goes into sex and dating. It doesn't just happen. There's physical grooming, new clothes and lingerie, perfume, a tidy house, and clean sheets. We want to make the best impression and be desirable and in doing so, we are feeding into the idea of 24-hour foreplay. We are turning ourselves on in the process. We are aware of our bodies, how they feel and we open our minds to the thought of pleasure. We may masturbate more because thinking about a new lover and being in a sense of anticipation feeds our desire for sex. Psychologists point out that being in a state of limerance is a major boost for your self-esteem too and makes you feel attractive and desired.

When limerance wears off, the sexual side of your relationship may be more challenging. What often happens is that a couple realise they don't have a strong enough emotional connection to sustain the relationship, or, as Corwin points out: 'If that's not the case, if we do want to have a deeper, lasting sexual intimacy with this person, then we have to let go of some romantic fantasies and embrace some realistic changes.'

'Women release more oxytocin than men so we have a strong need for an emotional connection as well as a physical one.'

Responsive desire

Rosemary Basson, Professor in Psychiatry, Obstetrics and Gynaecology at the University of British Columbia suggests that responsive desire is a more realistic model, which fits most of our sexual experiences. It is the notion that desire can be nurtured and reignited with practice and intention. Despite the physical differences in our make up – women have lower testosterone levels than men and therefore may not feel the urge to have sex in the same way as men do – we can quickly get there with the right circumstance and approach.

Often, kissing and massage and a sensual environment will lead to further intimacy once we have tuned into our bodies. In other words, we can generate feelings of desire by seeking out things that turn us on and make us want sex – lesbian porn, erotica, sensual experiences and fantasising. You need to exercise your brain as well as your body to prime it for sex. See Jack Morin's excellent book *The Erotic Mind* for more on this topic.

Corwin's view is that this is an empowering state of mind because it means we have a choice about how sexy we want to feel and we can make it happen. It is a team effort. 'Intentionality is the way to sustain sexual intimacy in a long-term relationship'. This increases your chances of happiness in a relationship and a relationship that lasts. It's not so much about 'compatibility' but willingness on both sides to give it a go.

You can set that intention at the start of a new relationship or have regular MOTs to tune in, see where things are between you and get things back on track. Accept that libido does wane and is cyclical at various times – we're all busy people and have various demands on us for our time and energy but if something is important and we're willing, we will make time for it.

Exercise

You can do this on your own first and then share the answers with your partner. Write down your answers to the following questions:

- What are your expectations and values around sex and intimacy?

- Who initiates sex the majority of the time and are you happy with that? Does one of you fall into the seducer role?

- How much time do you spend apart? Is there enough 'separateness' between you to ensure that desire has room to grow? Couples who spend all their time together often 'merge' and find it difficult to sustain physical desire and intimacy.

- Do you both masturbate and fantasise independently or seek pleasurable experiences individually?

- What type of physical stimulation brings you to orgasm when you masturbate?

'Accept that libido does wane and is cyclical at various times – we're all busy people and have various demands on us for our time and energy but if something is important and we're willing, we will make time for it.'

▨ Is there anything new you'd like to try with your partner?

Intimacy

Joanne Marrow PhD, and class instructor at Vulva University says: 'Intimacy means the mutual sharing of thoughts and ideas, emotions, touch, and psychic and energetic connections. We experience intimacy differently as we mature and understand that there are many levels of intimacy.' Intimacy is learned behaviour and often, people who haven't learned how to be intimate are seen as 'immature'.

She explains that psychologists use the metaphor of peeling the layers of an onion to describe the revelation of deepening intimacy. For it to develop we need to have a sense of trust, which may come in stages. 'Intimacy is desirable and gives us a sense of companionship, place, recognition, support, comfort and confidence. Yet, simultaneously, intimacy can feel demanding, frightening, unbalancing, controlling and threatening.' She says that people say they desire intimacy but when the chance arises to self-reveal, they often flee.

The resolution to this lies in self-love and acceptance. 'The person who fears intimacy does not value herself and has not searched out and consciously acknowledged and developed her fine qualities'. It's about low self-esteem and so she recommends falling in love with yourself and being your own best friend. Also know that developing intimacy is a life-long pursuit and to take it easier on ourselves – not all of the lessons may be with the same person. 'Your sense of intimacy will develop as both of you practise and learn more communication skills. Communication skills are learned. If you are both sincere in a desire for intimacy; you can seek workshops, practise groups, books and therapy to be a better communicator.'

Playwork

Marrow suggests two exercises to help you develop intimacy and a stronger energetic connection:

- Sit in silence and hold hands for a while noticing how it feels and the warmth that passes between you. You can choose to visualise your heart energy moving through your body to your partner's.

- Next time you have sex see if you can keep your eyes open when you orgasm. She explains that this will change the quality of the sex – it is you at your most vulnerable and open.

Mismatched libidos

Quite often one partner will have a higher sex drive than the other so it's about sensitivity, awareness and finding a solution that makes you both happy. Vibrators are also very useful as you need to have your own erotic life as well as the one you share with a lover . . . here are a few of the comments I received:

'My libido is slightly higher. Turning me on only takes a kiss or a naughty comment.' (Robyn, 21, Manchester).

'I usually have a higher sex drive than my partners. I think about sex a lot, and it doesn't take much to turn me on. I have been this way since my early teens onwards with a few dips during late pregnancy and after giving birth.' (Lorraine, 45, Kent).

'My libido is higher than my GF's. She only has to look at me in a certain way and it does it for me. My own imagination can turn me on when triggered by something. I use lesbian porn too. My GF doesn't but she knows I get off on it. Having kids means that you need to be careful when being intimate.' (JB, 37, Leeds).

'Sex is a very significant part of my life and relationship. My partner and I have boon to BDSM dyke play parties and we have a variety of sex toys. We both love and enjoy sex but would like to have more in our (monogamous) relationship, we can go weeks without having sex but we are always affectionate and intimate: lots of kissing and caressing even if no sex. The reason for infrequent sex has a lot to do with how sensitive we are to each other's moods and life stresses. If one of us has PMT, or is stressed at work, or is feeling tired we make sure we don't pressure each other into being sexual. That said, even during these times, if one makes an overture there is a 50% chance it will lead further.

'I think libido and initiating sex is a significant factor of any relationship – perhaps even more so in a lesbian one where both partners are trying to be 'understanding' and 'considerate'. We can always talk about sex and reassure each other that the affection and desire (which is always there) are what are really important. Sex is very meaningful to both of us and we value it as a huge part of our relationship. If there was no sex or sexual attraction at all, we wouldn't be in the relationship.' (Anna, 39, Devon).

'Sex is an active part of my life and my relationship. I'm very happy with it. The average frequency is once a day as my partner and I both have high libido. There's always lots of variety – we have been to various exciting places to do it in public, outside, etc. Communication plays a large part when we make love.' (Robyn, 21, Manchester).

'It's kind of an unspoken agreement that if one of us wants sex, we do it, knowing that it'll be good once we get going even if it wasn't originally on the agenda for right then. My wife had cancer during our first year together, and if anything, this made us more sexual, even during her treatment, as it made the worries fade for a while. I'm currently in early menopause according to my doctor, but it hasn't affected our sex life yet.' (Jo, 40, Hastings).

'Due to the fact that I have only been out for two years, I have a very high lesbian libido (my husband thought I was frigid and told me so – often!). However, my GF has been out since 17 and is not as highly sexed as me, but we get round it with compromise and understanding. I know when she prefers sex (morning) and when she is most horny (right before her period).' (Justine, 42, Middlesex).

'We have similar libido, me slightly less than her, but we seem to mismatch (we both want to be 'taken' which leads to nothing happening!). We have discussed that we have less sex than we'd like to, but it's not changed the status quo. Often when we have sex she will follow a stereotypical gradual crescendo pattern, which is often antithetical to what my body desires. I get off on whole body orgasm, which often means penetrate me and hold still whereas her inclination is to frig me faster and faster, often neglecting my vaginal area and bringing me (yawn) to a clitoral orgasm. I have issues with this cos, quite frankly, I can do that myself, much more efficiently!

'I have spent years celibate. I have enjoyed outrageous sex parties. I often enjoy a full body massage more than sex though I'm gobsmacked that my lover doesn't think to break the rules and fuck me while she's at it. I generally have to fantasise to cum during a clitoral orgasm when we have sex, and it usually involves her being fucked by my 'ideal man' whilst she fucks me. As a teenager, I was always instigating sexual games with my peers and broke lots of rules, some of which I feel bad about now. My libido totally vanishes sometimes . . . power and control turn me on. My short-term lovers have had those qualities, but they never worked out long term and when I got to 33, single and [having experienced] two recent heartbreaks, I put my heart aside and went out and found someone 'suitable'. A sad story to some, a mature story to others, an untold story to my lover!' (Cathie, 36, Lancashire).

Summing Up

- There are lots of myths around lesbian relationships and female sexuality. 'Lesbian bed death' is the notion that lesbian couples don't have as much sex or feel desire in a long-term relationship, in comparison to heterosexual and gay couples; that lesbian relationships are more emotionally driven, passion and stability aren't compatible and that our sexual urges decline after menopause. It is true that some lesbian relationships are more 'best friends' than lovers but this can also apply to long-term heterosexual relationships. The challenge is to keep the sexual energy flowing between you and this starts with your relationship to self.

- Take a 'sexual history' from your first lover to your current relationship. Look at the good and the bad experiences and what you've learned about yourself and your needs/desires over the years. What do you want now from a relationship? How important is sex and intimacy to you and what steps do you take to prioritise it? How much time do you allow in your day for pleasure and reconnection with self and your partner?

- The idea of 24-hour foreplay is recommended by sex therapists as a way to build and maintain a flow of energy. Keep an erotic diary and find ways to do stuff that makes you feel passionate and alive – physical activities, food, exercise, yoga, and ways to turn yourself on through erotica, writing about sex, fantasy, porn and masturbation.

- There are two types of sexual desire – spontaneous (the early stages of passion/lust) and responsive, which is more applicable to long-term relationships and focuses on willingness and intention to have a fulfilling erotic life. It's about actively planning things to do alone and together to maintain your drive and desire.

Chapter Three

The Female Body

We live in a culture that emphasises an ideal of the female body and puts pressure on older women to change, improve and 'keep up' with younger women physically. For lesbians this pressure can be greater – look at the representation of an ideal gay women in TV shows such as The L-Word for example: attractive and just the right type of 'femme' or 'androgynous'. If you are butch there's also a certain look and expectation to fit into. Many women reject those labels and just want to be healthy and feel comfortable in their own skin without the external pressure to fit into a box of what a 'woman' should look like or how she should act. Many lesbians have tattoos and piercings as a form of reclaiming their bodies, identities and as a form of self-expression.

Body confidence

Sex writer Dr Pam Spurr did a survey about body image and found that the average woman has low levels of body confidence, which can affect our sexual confidence. She has a few pointers in her book *Sex Academy*:

- Visualisation – seeing yourself as the sexiest person in the room and holding that thought throughout the day.

- Stripping for yourself in front of a mirror – practise doing it in a submissive persona (i.e. eyes downcast) and a dominant one – play with that power exchange. Which feels most natural and empowering?

- Burlesque classes are all about getting in touch with your body, whatever your shape or size.

- Self-massage – focus on the bits you don't like and work on self-acceptance. Observe any negative thoughts that come up as you touch those areas and let the thoughts go.

- Daily exercise – commit to doing something that gets you moving to help raise endorphins.

- Self-pleasuring – do it regularly to keep that connection between mind and body.

- Look after yourself physically – dentist, hair appointments, clothes, make-up if you wear it, treatments.

Writer and blogger Holly Moyseenko (www.mysexprofessor.com) says she's not someone who hates the way she looks, but she doesn't love her body most days. She is getting better at it after living with people who are immensely comfortable in their own bodies. 'Seeing people's naked bodies on a regular basis made me stop viewing my body as unattractive. When I explained to another friend that I wanted to change how I viewed myself, he suggested that I think of what my body does for me and try thanking it. Every day I try to pick at least one body part, and be thankful for it. After five months of actively working on my body image, there is some improvement, it's definitely not an overnight change, and even though I no longer live with my clothing-optional friends, I am still actively working on improving how I view myself.'

Anna Samson, 39, blogs at *Sexy at Any Size*. She writes erotica and encourages women to explore, evolve, express and enjoy their unique sexual selves through workshops and courses at *The Ladygarden Project*. Here are her thoughts on 'Radical Desire':

'One thing I couldn't hide though was the size of my body. I'd always been big despite climbing on and off the yo-yo dieting wagon. My upbringing had taught me that being pretty equated to being slim. I was fat and I was frigging myself: I was failing at being pretty and at being good.

'To add even further to my list of supposed misdemeanours, I found my body erotic. Looking at it, touching it, smelling and tasting it all added to my self-arousal. I got off on myself.

'I wasn't immune to days of poor body image, trying to change my body through yet another diet, or wishing my legs were more like the sexy legs in the Pretty Polly adverts, but somewhere, deep down, I had the sense that my self-esteem was more important to me than a slim body, and that my sex life would suffer if I stopped turning myself on.

'I've been blessed with a healthy libido and I attribute a large part of this to being able to enjoy my body sexually. Whether on my own, or with a partner, sexual desire begins with self-desire: if I don't believe I'm sexy why would I believe my body should be having sex? But I know that this goes against those two earlier rules (good girls don't; pretty equals slim). And I know that sometimes – too often – people judge their body to be unworthy of feeling sexy because there is something about its appearance they don't like. Be this the size of their breasts, or the size of their belly, the inability to be able to enjoy and desire that body part (or often parts) – to feel sexy at any size or shape – means that their sexual selves are limited, repressed, or simply not fully realised.

'Personally, I choose to view my body and my sexuality as gifts. Sure I could reject those gifts but, without the receipt, I don't have the option to return or exchange them. I have two options: ignore the gifts and leave them hidden in the bottom of a cupboard somewhere, forgotten and unappreciated; or be grateful for my gifts, enjoy and make use of them.

'I choose the latter.

'I also choose to reclaim the constructs of my childhood: I choose to be a good girl who does, and I choose to be a pretty woman who can take pleasure in her fat body.

'Is that so radical?'

Exercise

Use a full-length mirror and a smaller hand-held one to have a really good look at your body. Simply observe it when you are naked, warm and alone. Notice any negative thoughts or judgements that come up. Try to see yourself objectively before zoning in on grey hairs, wrinkles or saggy bits. What do you like about yourself? Which bits are strong, sensual and sensitive to touch? What message do you send to yourself when you look into your eyes? Is it a sense of appreciation, softness and love, or do you avoid really looking at yourself? This can be quite an emotional exercise when you do it repeatedly and you may feel some shifts in how you feel about it. I found it quite difficult to start with – five minutes seemed like an eternity but it's got easier the more I do it.

Take the smaller mirror and have a good look at your genital area. Gently part your labia and notice how it feels, folds and sits. Lift the hood of your clitoris and have a look at the nub, see if you can feel the clitoral legs running down beneath your labia. Give yourself a self-massage using lube and notice how sensitive your vagina is when you insert a finger, massage your perineum and anal area too.

Female sexual response cycle

In the 1950s, sexologists Masters & Johnson identified four stages of sexual response from arousal to post-orgasm:

- Excitement (Arousal) – When the brain responds to a kinky thought or touch, triggering an increase in blood in the body. Your heart rate goes up, breathing quickens and your body flushes. Nipples become erect and the labia majora flatten out, swelling in size. The labia minora also get bigger and the clitoris has its own mini erection. Your vagina balloons and lubricates in preparation for penetration, your uterus lifts up and the anal muscles contract.

- Plateau – This is the period just before orgasm when excitement is peaking. It's a shorter phase in women than men. The vagina fully opens and the clitoral glans retracts under its hood. Blood congests giving you that full sensation in the genitals that need release via orgasm.

- Orgasm – A muscular release where the accumulated blood flows backwards stimulating the nerve pathways. It feels expansive and your whole body opens up. It can also have a mental element – like you are letting go and relaxing. Post-orgasm you may feel clear, focused and have increased energy levels. Use the moments post-orgasm to focus on something you want to manifest that day. Orgasmic contractions come at 0.8-second intervals (according to Masters & Johnson) and in women, it lasts around 15 seconds. Women can experience multiple orgasms too, by taking the focus off the clitoris post-orgasm and stimulating the G-spot then going back to the clitoris a minute or so later – something to experiment with.

- Resolution – Post-orgasm your muscles relax and blood pressure and breathing go back to normal. The hormone prolactin is released, which makes you feel happy and relaxed. Women may not have 'blue balls' (where men get that frustrated ache in their testicles if they don't orgasm) but we have something similar – an accumulation of blood in the genital area can feel uncomfortable for a while if it isn't released through orgasm.

Since the 1950s other sexologists have added further stages to the response model. Helen Singer Kaplan thought that 'desire' should be a precursor to 'arousal', and in the 1980s Joann Loutan added 'willingness' – i.e. even if you have no physical desire for sex then a willingness to just do it helps women to get into the groove. This echoes what we said earlier about responsive desire and, in a way; it's about taking responsibility for our sex lives and orgasms. We rarely feel like going to the gym but always feel better afterwards and are glad we made the effort.

So, we have a sexual response model to work with although as Felice Newman, author of *The Whole Lesbian Sex Book* points out, you're unlikely to time it or be aware of the different stages in the heat of the moment. What you can do is cultivate awareness – why not put a clock in the bedroom so you have an idea of how long it takes you to orgasm?

Loss of libido

'My partner is five years older than me and we have friends who are now in their 50s. I do wonder what will happen as menopause approaches. Friends tell us it has put their sex lives on hold. I really hope we can find a way to still enjoy sex and sexuality despite the mood swings, hot flushes, etc. I would appreciate information on being in a relationship where both partners are going through the menopause. Navigating PMT in a lesbian relationship is tough enough!' (Anna, 39, Devon)

The good news, says Glenda Corwin, is that studies show a drop in libido isn't always age-related or linked to menopause. It can happen to women in their 20s. One study followed 326 women aged 35-47 for four years and found that less than one-third said they had decreased libido. Hormonal changes aren't the only reason for a drop in libido – it can be linked to other factors: self-esteem, relationship issues or work or family stress. Often older women report a rise in sex drive after menopause (testosterone levels naturally rise as oestrogen falls) but it's the physical issues that need addressing – vaginal dryness being a common one. You can use extra lubricant and also try a natural progesterone cream such as Serenity Wellspring or explore bio-identical hormones if you don't want to take conventional HRT. See *Menopause: The Essential Guide* (Need2Know) for further information.

It's important to maintain physical intimacy with yourself post-menopause and there are things you can do to 'reinvigorate' the vaginal area – herbalist Susun S Weed suggests having a daily orgasm for a week if your libido has fallen or you're experiencing vaginal dryness. Herbal medicine can work wonders with libido. I used it to help with this and amenorrhoea in my 20s/30s. A weekly yoga class will also exercise the pelvic area and maintain blood flow – vital for sexual arousal and orgasms as well as giving you more headspace and relaxation. Writer and broadcaster Jo Fairley swears by her weekly yoga class and has published a new book on yoga for the over 50s.

If you are concerned about your libido see your GP first off for a general health check to rule out any other problems – thyroid, testosterone levels, etc. It's also helpful to speak to a nutritionist as there are many foods that will boost libido – raw chocolate, oily fish and maca are fantastic aphrodisiacs. Read Marrena Lindberg's book *The Orgasmic Diet* for ideas.

Get to know your own 'body map' – here's the lowdown on your lady garden:

Your genital region encompasses the clitoris, vulva, vagina, labia, urethral opening, perineum and anus. The mirror exercise we talked about earlier is worth doing and you can use a speculum if you want to look at your G-spot. Gently insert it after an orgasm and use the mirror to look at the top wall of your vagina. Some women like to shave their pubic hair – it makes oral sex a bit smoother and can increase sensitivity. You can also get a better look at your labia and clitoris.

'It's important to maintain physical intimacy with yourself post-menopause and there are things you can do to "reinvigorate" the vaginal area.'

The clitoris ('polishing the pearl')

The clitoris is your pleasure centre – it contains 8,000 nerve endings and is the only organ in your body designed purely for pleasure. As we've recently discovered (thanks to Helen O'Connell's research on cadavers) it extends much further back into the body than we thought. It resembles a wishbone – the nub sits outside the body at the top of your labia and the crura (legs) extend back around 8cm inside the pelvic area. This means that all orgasms are clitoral in origin. Two bulbs cup the crura, sitting underneath a bit like testicles. Masturbation guru Betty Dodson has a video showing the internal parts of the clitoris on her website, www.dodsonandross.com.

What's fascinating is that the size and placement of the clitoris is different in women – no two are the same size or in the same location just as no two penises or labia are the same shape or size. We're unique. Women will also require a different kind of stimulation according to how they are wired (their pelvic nerve placement) so it's a case of starting again with each new lover. If direct clitoral stimulation is too much, diffuse the sensation by stimulating it through fabric or using a vibrator around the area – see what feels best – many women like a vibe across the entire clitoral area.

The ladies at Sh! Womenstore say: 'Just as where we enjoy being touched is individual to us, so is the kind of touch we enjoy on our clitorises. Some women can only cope with the lightest of fingertip strokes, whereas others need the zingy intensity of a vibrator's buzz on their clitorises to get them off. Different levels of intensity can produce different kinds of orgasms – the slow build-up of feather-light touches will often result in a shuddering orgasm whereas firmer sensations may give you a short, sharp blast of an orgasm. All kinds of touches, just like all kinds of orgasms are worth pursuing.'

Given that it's such a powerhouse for women and a source of intense pleasure, it's crazy to think, as Felice Newman points out, that it has been entirely disregarded by the medical profession. The clitoris is not produced in full detail in the medical bible *Gray's Anatomy*, which means that surgeons doing hysterectomies and other pelvic operations may inadvertently damage the nerve area that gives a woman sexual pleasure, without knowing.

'The clitoris is your pleasure centre – it contains 8,000 nerve endings and is the only organ in your body designed purely for pleasure.'

Labia

The labia majora (outer lips) and minora (inner lips) are very sensitive and contain sweat glands to aid the release of pheromones (chemicals produced by the body that help attract a mate). The labia minora protect the clitoris, urethra and vagina and provide extra stimulation if fingering or fisting a woman. The inner and outer labia are homologous to the mouth – think of your inner and outer lips and how they respond to kissing. In the movie *Sleeping Beauty*, the lead character is asked to paint her lips the same colour as her labia before a play scene. She has no idea what the right colour is and chooses red, much to mistress' displeasure. The other woman chooses a more muted colour and off they go. It made me look at my make-up bag in a whole new light!

A drop or two of ON Arousal Cream (natural zingy oils) will increase clitoral and labial sensitivity for around 15 minutes. Wonder stuff!

Urethral opening

This is the tube connecting the bladder to the genital area so that fluid can be passed from the body. In women it is found just above the entrance to the vagina and is about 1.5-2 inches long compared to 8 inches for men (the male urethra – 'meatus' – is located at the tip of the penis). It has a basic function but it can also be a source of sexual pleasure in men and women as the urethra is packed with nerve endings and responds to stimulation externally and internally. Men ejaculate as well as pee from the urethral opening and women can also ejaculate seminal fluid from it during orgasm; it is clear and slightly thicker than urine. Try touching it gently with your finger or tongue initially to see how she likes it. You can also stimulate the urethra using Urethral Sounds (medical devices made of glass or metal) – a BDSM practice that involves gently probing and widening the urethra for sexual pleasure.

Vagina

The vagina is shaped like a barrel, muscular, and, like the diaphragm, it closes flat when you're unaroused so it's not a 'hole' as such. During sexual arousal and childbirth it will expand to accommodate. The first inch or two is the most sensitive area for a finger or G-spot toy. Shallow penetration with a tongue or finger will feel good and you can stimulate the G-spot and A-spot (on her front vaginal wall) once she is turned on. Some women love deep penetration that hits the cervix, the neck of your womb during a period or when they are really excited. Like any muscle, it deserves lots of TLC with regular touch and pelvic exercise. The more you masturbate the more lubrication your glands will produce meaning that arousal happens that little bit faster.

PC muscle

This is a hammock of muscles to hold your internal reproductive organs in place. Your PC muscle also increase the sensitivity of your G-spot and help orgasmic contractions so the stronger they are, the more intense your orgasms. Age, weight, gravity and childbirth all weaken PC muscle tone so it's vital as we get older to do daily exercise – it can be as simple as identifying your flow of urine and squeezing those muscles slowly and rapidly in succession, several times a day. Do it sitting down or standing in a queue. Do the same with your anal sphincter and make sure you relax the muscles properly after tightening.

There are various gadgets on the market to do the job for you and I'd use these in conjunction with manual exercise – it's important to feel what you are doing too and how the vagina changes and responds to the exercise over time. Don't expect quick results – it may take a few months to really feel a difference. I like Smart Balls, which you can wear during the day to tone you as you work/walk. They feel nice and can be a turn on too (see chapter 7 for more information).

G-spot

The G-spot isn't a specific area but a sensitive pleasure zone 1-2 inches inside the vagina along the upper wall. Jaiya and Jon Hanauer (The New School of Erotic Touch) point out that every woman's G-spot is different because we have varying levels of sensitivity based on biomechanics, biochemistry, emotional development and scar tissue. Hanauer says: 'The G-spot has a head, body and tail that make up the entire area. The head is the urethral opening. You can see this just above the vaginal opening. It is a tiny hole from which urine or ejaculate is expelled. The body of the G-spot is located on the front wall of the vagina if a woman is lying down. This is a tube of erectile tissue that surrounds the urethra and fills with fluid during arousal. The important thing to note is that women have higher concentrations of this sensitive tissue in three different areas. For the majority of women, most of the erectile tissue is near the opening of the vagina, the second is further inside near the G-spot tail, and the third area is in the centre of the urethral sponge.

'Your PC muscle also increase the sensitivity of your G-spot and help orgasmic contractions so the stronger they are, the more intense your orgasms.'

The G-spot tail is about 3-4 inches inside the vaginal cavity on the front wall (also known as the A-spot or anterior fornix zone).

Perineum

This is the area of stretchy skin between the vagina and anus. It is an often ignored hot spot in men and women so worth massaging and exploring with lube and during oral sex. Midwives recommend massaging it prior to childbirth (using your fingers internally and externally) to gently stretch the skin so that it won't tear during childbirth. This is a lovely thing for you and your partner to do during pregnancy to involve her in the birth preparation.

Anus

The anus is crammed with nerve endings – far more than the vagina, which is why anal sex and rimming can feel so good. It's also still a little taboo and many women are squeamish about the thought of encountering poo. Relax. You won't. Fecal matter is stored higher up in the colon/rectum. The anus is around 1-2 inches long and leads to the rectum. Try rimming using a dental dam for safety and gentle finger massage externally before you massage inside. Use plenty of lube (and reapply) as the area doesn't self-lubricate. Done slowly and with enough lubrication, anal sex shouldn't hurt but it's not something you can rush. There are two sphincters – the first you can relax and the second will involuntarily tighten when a finger or toy penetrates it so just wait, hold it there until your partner (or self) relaxes fully for stimulation to continue. There are lots of great anal toys on the market – beads, plugs and vibrators to give different sensations. What can feel fantastic is the sensation of anal beads being slowly pulled out when you orgasm – it will heighten the sensation.

Sh! Womenstore in London runs workshops on anal play and there are lots of great books on the subject – see Tristan Taormino's and Jack Morin's.

Talking to your doctor about sex

Stonewall's Health Report for Lesbian and Bisexual Women (2008) states that lesbian women are more likely to smoke and drink heavily than women in general. They are less likely to have had a smear test and more likely to have had breast cancer. Levels of self-harm, depression, anxiety and suicide are higher than the general population. They have also had negative experiences within healthcare and don't always come out to their GP. Less than half of women in the study had been screened for an STI, and 15% of lesbian and bisexual women over 25 had never had a smear test.

It's vital to have Pap smear every three years in the UK – it can save your life. It's also important to have STI check-ups when you start a new sexual relationship, particularly if it's non-monogamous.

If you don't feel your doctor is gay-friendly then you are within your rights to switch and find someone you are happy with. The UK is developing polyclinics – centres where you can access a GP and sexual health centre under one roof. I had an email this week about a new LGBT health and wellbeing centre, which is opening in Birmingham's Southside district in January 2013, to meet the healthcare needs of the lesbian, gay, bisexual and transgender community and hopefully this model will follow suit in other cities around the UK.

Pap smears aren't fun but you can make the process more comfortable by taking control. Dorrie Lane suggests asking the nurse to warm the speculum first, inserting it yourself, and asking for a small mirror so you can see the cervix and inside the vagina (if you wish to). Use plenty of lube and you can ask for mitts to go over the stirrups to make them more comfortable – anything that helps to make the process quicker and more comfortable for you. I live in hope that the day comes when we have porn and sex toys available for use in sexual health clinics!

For a deeper understanding of how your body works she recommends reading *A New View of a Woman's Body* by the Women's Feminist Health Centre. I'd also recommend Vulva University's free course in OB/GYN, which you can access via their website, www.houseochicks.com.

'If you don't feel your doctor is gay-friendly then you are within your rights to switch and find someone you are happy with.'

Summing Up

- Women are under increasing pressure to conform to body image ideals – the media's representation of the right type of 'femme' or 'butch'. Many women have body confidence issues, which can affect sexual confidence and self-expression. It's about finding a happy medium: being healthy and happy with your body and making changes where you can, taking care of yourself and finding ways to express your sexuality in a meaningful way – clothes, tattoos, piercings are all forms of self-expression. You can work on body image through workshops, for example, Nina Grunfeld's Life Clubs and Anna Sampson's The Lady Garden project. Challenge how you see your body by focusing on the positive, your health and all that it does for you.

- There are four stages of sexual response from arousal to post-orgasm, as defined by sex researchers Masters & Johnson in the 1950s. Desire and willingness have since been added to this model. Be aware of your sexual responses – how long does it take you to orgasm, for example, alone and with a partner? How much foreplay do you need?

- Loss of libido isn't always age-related or down to menopause. It can affect women in their 20s too, and is often related to non-physical factors – self-esteem, stress and relationship issues. Address the physical side first with your doctor and then explore psychological factors.

- Sexual health is often neglected in LGBT relationships. There are lots of health inequalities within the health service but things are changing, with more polyclinics on offer in the UK and dedicated LGBT health and wellbeing centres. Find a GP you are happy with and take in a list of questions you have. It's important to have regular STI tests and Pap smears, even if you don't sleep with men.

Need2Know

Chapter Four

Self-Pleasure

We all do it. But, we don't talk about it. In a recent interview with Huffington Post, bestselling author of *Lace*, Shirley Conran commented: 'what is not yet discussed by either sex is female masturbation, which remains a taboo subject. Men think it is, a) filthy, b) an affront to masculinity and to themselves personally. Nice women don't do it.

'But we do.

'On the other hand, male masturbation is a) only natural, b) provides a healthy relief before marriage or when a woman is not available, such as in prisons, warships, tents and tanks or anywhere, anytime, when alone and unobserved.

'The French writer Colette once wrote that a good lover is one that can do it better than you can. Maybe that's why men don't like the idea of a woman being able to please herself. This is one perception that hasn't changed a bit in 30 years – both in bed and out of it.'

In The Kinsey Report (1950s) 62% of women said they masturbate regularly. By the 1970s, post pill generation, Shere Hite's report on female sexuality had that figure at 82%. She revolutionised female sexuality by focusing on female pleasure and releasing women from the idea that they should be able to orgasm through penetrative sex alone. Although it's something most of us take pleasure from, we rarely talk about it (tips and techniques) with girlfriends or even partners for that matter. Which is a shame because it means we can get stuck in a rut, self-pleasuring in the same ways we learnt when younger, a way that enables us to orgasm quickly and quietly. This isn't a problem when we're alone but it can be incompatible with partner sex. Given that statistics show most women need prolonged clitoral stimulation to come, then it makes sense to revise our techniques over the years, try new things, as we do with new partners.

Maybe part of the issue is the word itself – 'masturbation' – hardly feminine, it has a brutal sound to it. As sex columnist Suzi Godson points out in *The Sex Book*: 'Only 10 years ago dictionaries defined the word "masturbation" as "self-abuse",' and explains that a Swiss physician SA Tissot (1728-97) is largely responsible. 'He devised a theory that sex (and especially masturbation) could starve the brain and the nervous system, eventually leading to madness and blindness. Backed by the church, the idea caught on, to the extent that in Victorian Britain, masturbation was considered to be a pathological perversion guaranteed to cause insanity'. It has taken a long time for this viewpoint to be reversed and for masturbation to be acknowledged as something that's good for us and fun. It is still controversial in many cultures. If the word makes you cringe substitute it for 'self-pleasure', 'autoeroticism' or something more fitting.

Health benefits

'Studies show that women who masturbate regularly have higher levels of desire, satisfaction and a better orgasm rate.'

According to The World Congress of Sexology: 'Sexual pleasure, including autoeroticism (masturbation), is a source of physical, psychological, intellectual and spiritual wellbeing'. Studies show that women who masturbate regularly have higher levels of desire, satisfaction and a better orgasm rate. It releases endorphins and strengthens your pelvic floor. Your body gets used to it and produces more natural lubricant. 'It makes you want more sex', say sex writers Em & Lo. It develops your sex sensitivity and trains your nerves to respond more efficiently. It boosts your self-esteem, enabling you to learn how to love the look, feel, smell and shape of your body.

Masturbation also:

- Increases self-intimacy and sexual confidence. You know how to give yourself pleasure and how your body responds to different kinds of touch and stimulation. You learn your 'body map' as Vulva University describe it, so you can tell a new lover what gives you pleasure. It also makes you produce more pheromones (our body's natural chemicals) and makes you more attractive to others. I can tell when a woman is in touch with her sexuality because she radiates it from every pore. It gives you more energy, openness, and enables you to communicate better with others. You walk and talk your sexuality, and that is a powerful thing in terms of creativity and getting things done.

46

- It keeps the vagina and PC muscles toned and lubricated. Clitoral stimulation is great but you also need internal stimulation using your fingers, dildo or vibrator regularly to stimulate powerful intra-vaginal spots, as we'll discuss later.

- It relaxes your mind and body, stimulates creativity, and helps you let go of emotions and move on.

- It improves your health if you are physically ill and can't have penetrative partner sex.

- Pain relief – I haven't found a better natural cure for PMS, period cramps and headaches.

- The best solution for mismatched libidos – when one partner wants more sex than the other. It dissolves that sexual tension and allows us to pace ourselves in terms of sexual needs.

- 'It makes you a better lover,' says Dorrie Lane. 'When you know what pleasures your body, when you experiment with different techniques and touches, you broaden your erotic senses. You begin to learn your erotic "body map". You may even discover things about yourself you were not aware of. You will certainly learn what areas of your body are more responsive to touch. As we age, our bodies change and regular masturbation helps us to adapt to those changes. Orgasms vary with different touch and technique and this is important to be aware of. It is especially important to share these changes with your partner.'

Stuck in a rut?

Shere Hite classified the main masturbation styles in The New Hite Report. They are:

- On your back – hands on your clitoris

- On your stomach – against an object

- Pressing your thighs together

- Using water pressure e.g. a shower

- Vaginal insertion – toy or hand

Do you always do it in the same way, for same length of time?

Do you rely on toys? Use the same fantasy? Stop yourself after one orgasm?

If that's the case, shake things up a bit. What would you like to experience? Anal orgasm? Ejaculation? Tantric orgasm? Aim to wake up all of your senses for a longer period than usual. 'Don't try to match your sexuality to a male. We need to take our time,' says Betty Dodson, orgasm doctor and author of best-selling book *Self-loving For One*. Watching each other masturbate is a great way to learn about each other's bodies and takes the pressure off mismatched libidos e.g. if one of you has a higher sexual drive, or is going through a period of illness. 'It's also okay to finish off the job if you haven't had an orgasm and your partner has,' says Dodson.

Practise! Couples therapist Lonnie Barbach suggests an hour a day for six weeks to get your body used to and expecting that level of stimulation. An hour a day might be pushing it but aim for 15 minutes a day and slowly build it up, incorporating your PC exercises. The effects will be more noticeable over time as vaginal strength and sensitivity increases. It's also worth investing in a set of love balls – spherical balls made of silicone or glass that you wear internally to stimulate the muscles while you work. Some brands are quieter than others – I like Teneo Smartballs, and they feel pretty good too.

'In order to get the most out of solo sex you need to reverse the goal of orgasm and make the process the most important thing, don't rush to orgasm,' says Suzi Godson.

Exercise

Giving yourself an hour of pleasure is a simple enough idea but not always that easy in practice. Put it in the diary and stick to it as life has a habit of taking over. You may find it easy to climax in ten minutes with a vibrator but the challenge here is to give yourself continuous pleasure and permission to stay up there with your energy, so that multiple orgasms are possible and you awaken all of your senses. This is what makes a full body (tantric) orgasm more likely. Bring in breast massage using oils to increase sensitivity (see Taoist breast massage exercise on the following page), and explore your clitoris, G-spot, anus and perineum. Take a few deep breaths and move your pelvis around before you start masturbating.

> 'In order to get the most out of solo sex you need to reverse the goal of orgasm and make the process the most important thing, don't rush to orgasm.'
>
> Suzi Godson, sex columnist

Using your voice – making as much noise as you can, as you get more excited, will make it easier to let go. Over time, bring in new toys to play with and experiment with holding back – stopping as your orgasm builds, allowing it to dissipate and resuming again. Doing this seven times (or as close as you can get!) before you allow yourself to dissolve into orgasm will give you 'the excruciating pleasure of a full body orgasm', says orgasm coach Dr Lisa Turner. She describes it as an endless wave of pleasure that fills your entire being, sex at soul level.

Taoist breast massage

'Breast massage increases the flow of chi to your breasts. You can do it on a daily basis. It clears stagnant chi and ensures that chi, blood and lymph keeps flowing. In addition, massaging the breasts is a natural way to increase and balance oestrogen levels in your body. For women who do not have much sensitivity in their breasts, massaging them can make them more sensitive and receptive,' says Uta Demontis, a sex and relationship coach based in London (www.manawa.co.uk).

Dr Rachel Abrams in her book *The Multi-Orgasmic Woman* (with Mantak Chia) recommends 'thinking of the breasts primarily as a symbol for nurturing yourself. For many women, this may seem counter-intuitive since we often think of our breasts in relationship to providing for others (our baby's or our partner's pleasure)'.

I like doing this exercise in the bath:

※ Warm up your hands by rubbing them together.

※ Place your palms over your breasts and smile into your heart. Feel love, joy and happiness in your heart. Then smile into your breasts. Send thoughts of appreciation and love to your breasts.

※ First massage slowly from inside your breasts upwards and around to the outside. This direction disperses chi and eliminates stagnant chi.

※ Then reverse the direction and massage slowly from the outside of your breasts to the inside. This direction brings more energy into our breasts.

■ Gently open and close your yoni (vagina) as you massage your breasts. Circle at least 36 times each direction. Traditional Taoist texts recommend 36-360 circles. Enjoy about five minutes massaging your breasts.

G-spot inter-vagina self-massage

Val Guin is a sought-after massage therapist based in LA. She teaches women how to do G-spot massage for health and wellness, which she calls the 'G-spot Inter-Vaginal Self Massage'. In an interview with *CURVE* magazine she said she aims to demystify the stigma attached to the vagina, and encourages women to openly talk about sex to educate about the health benefits of the G-spot massage. It can help some of the most common daily ailments like back pain and sexual problems. 'The bottom line is that they [women] do too much, give too much, don't recognise and are not conscious of their own personal needs. Women tend to be caretakers. What I've found is that when women take care of themselves, they can still be as caring and loving to their partners, even more so because they will be out of pain, strong, light, joyful and basically enthusiastic about their life experience.'

'Massaging the G-spot with your finger will increase your orgasms, and give you an orgasm that comes from deep inside and rises through the body – the full body or tantric orgasm.'

She explains that massaging the G-spot with your finger will increase your orgasms, and give you an orgasm that comes from deep inside and rises through the body – the full body or tantric orgasm.

'Now the G-spot is just one area. There are other spots, called inter-vaginal points. This energy has been understood and used for thousands of years in all cultures around the world. Much of it can be traced back to the roots of Tantra, Taoism, the Shamans, Kahunas and healers. It is the most powerful energy we have and when directed it can increase a woman's overall wellness'. It is controversial for practitioners to be working on these points so she teaches women how to do the points on themselves.

'Many women believe that penetration is not necessary for a healthy sex life; this seems to be especially true in the lesbian community. This belief is not true. These inter-vaginal points are extremely powerful, in terms of orgasm and women's health and wellness. Lesbians could potentially have better orgasms and be healthier if they would learn to incorporate vaginal penetration into their sex lives. Healthy inter-vaginal points cause a healthier pelvis, spine elongation, which results in better posture, better energy, less discomfort of pain, better organ function so you have less menstrual and menopausal cramping, better bladder and bowel function, and it allows the pelvis to be in a better position for more fulfilling sex.'

So, where are the inter-vaginal points? Guin says they line the vagina and form harder and softer areas. Massaging the areas will decrease the tightness and tone the bits that need it, creating tissue balance.

How do we do it?

'The easiest way to do this is with a G-spot stimulator. Gently explore the tissue, you may or may not feel or understand how the tissue feels or how it is changing but you will still notice a difference in your overall wellbeing. Look for changes in your posture, your attitude and how you feel. For those of you wanting to really practise and understand that, you [should look] for tissue changes. When you find a spot that feels like it does not let you sink in gently, do not push hard; instead just gently hold the G-spot stimulator over the spot and allow it to melt into the area. If you find areas that seem overly soft, then again hold the G-spot stimulator over the area pressing very gently and you will feel the tissue begin to gain firmness. Use your breath to relax the body as you do these exercises and don't rush it. It takes time to work with your G-spot area and build muscle tone. It is something you can do on your own and with a partner – helping each other to discover new sensations.

Tantric massage

I also recommend booking a tantric massage for yourself and your partner. It is incredibly sensual to watch and will give you both new ideas for pleasuring. There is no expectation around returning the pleasure so all you have to do is submit and let it happen. Whether or not you choose to orgasm is up to you. It's about working with sexual energy to expand your mind and body. Once your body experiences something new physically it creates new neural pathways in the brain. You then have a muscle memory of it and it will be easier to recreate it. Here's a link to an article from RUDE magazine on tantric massage with Bara: www.rudemagazine.co.uk/features/why-we-need-to-be-touched.php.

Mutual masturbation

In Vulva University's e-course on masturbation, the tutor mentions Albert Ellis' PhD work on the subject, in which he talks about the sexual benefits of masturbation with a partner. 'You can be observed by a partner and bring yourself and your partner special arousal and satisfaction, you can learn about your own sexuality and by your partner's observations'. He also points out that we need to see the value in giving to ourselves before we can receive from another. In other words, become devoted to yourself. 'It is a form of self-expression so you may take more risks in life – be open to pleasure seeking and more adventurous sex'.

'Our G-spots are the ultimate in shareable pleasure parts,' says Violet Blue, author of *The Smart Girl's Guide to the G-spot*. 'Number one is that the G-spot's in an area that is often more easily accessed by a lover; the angle and the pressure many women find necessary to stimulate their spot's pleasure is often better accompanied by someone else. Another great reason, especially for G-spot newcomers, is that finding and learning about the G-spot can be both easier and more fun when you have a partner helping you figure out what you like. A G-spot adventure shared by two is an incredibly intimate adventure.'

See the help list for useful websites about self-pleasure techniques.

Summing Up

- 82% of women masturbate according to *The Hite Report on Female Sexuality*. However, unlike sex, we don't really talk about it. We don't swap tips and techniques, which means it's easy to stay doing the same thing to orgasm and get stuck in a style or pattern of pleasure that gets you off fast. That's okay but not every time you self-pleasure. As with sex, we need quickies and more languorous, tantric-style experiences. You can create new habits around masturbation through mutual exploration, reading more, talking about it more, watching DVDs (e.g. *The Art of Female Ejaculation* by Deborah Sundahl), accessing online seminars by Betty Dodson and learning more about our body's physical responses.

- Masturbation has numerous health benefits – it's a source of physical, psychological, intellectual and spiritual wellbeing. Women who self-pleasure regularly have higher levels of desire, satisfaction, and a better orgasm rate. It strengthens the pelvic floor and keeps the vagina lubricated. It also makes you a better lover. Aim to set aside an hour a day – or build up to this – to explore new forms of touch and toys. See if you can experience orgasm in different ways – keep going if you normally stop after the first clitoral orgasm. Try an anal toy while you masturbate or nipple clamps. See if you can have multiple orgasms.

- Regular breast massage increases the sensitivity in your breasts so they are more likely, over time, to bring you to orgasm through breast massage alone.

Chapter Five

Dating and Friendship

The lesbian scene

The online social network for lesbians, www.planet-london.com ran an online survey last year for the 200,000 lesbian and bisexual women based in the city. They wanted to find out more about women's social habits and needs, and had 717 responses to the survey. Here are the key points:

1. Women go out a lot, at least once a week, and do a range of social activities – a friend's house, pub or club, sports or social event, theatre, arts, comedy, gigs and festivals.

2. Soho is the main hub for central London activity aimed at the gay/lesbian market.

3. Most drink socially but it's not all they want to do. There's a need for daytime places to meet – cafés and non-alcoholic venues as many women feel this is lacking. Women enjoy a range of activities – cooking, book clubs, walking (and dog walking), coffee and cake, healthy living – Pilates and yoga classes, and creative arts. They also volunteer for various reasons: political, feminist activism, to give back and be a role model to other lesbians. Many women get involved in LGBT organisations like Stonewall and non-LGBT charities such as Childline.

4. Many women feel that lesbian events are often held in less than attractive venues around town, e.g. basements.

5. There's a general perception from the LGBT community that the 'scene' is aimed at single lesbians in their 20s-30s. However, many older women and couples still want to go out and meet people.

'There's a general perception from the LGBT community that the 'scene' is aimed at single lesbians in their 20s-30s. However, many older women and couples still want to go out and meet people.'

'London is unique [compared to other UK cities] because it's lost a lot of women's spaces, particularly chilled places such as cafés where you can go in the daytime,' says Naomi Bennett, co-founder of Planet London website. '95% of the lesbian scene is centred around alcohol and loud music so you can't actually talk to anyone.' Central London has lost a lot of LGBT events because of the high rents, which means organisers have to be a little bit more creative, hosting pop-up events and fringe stuff. Places such as the Candy Bar in Soho (recently bought out to save it from closure) are trendy and aimed at a younger crowd in their 20-30s, so how can you meet women if you aren't into that?

One way, says Bennett, is to go online. There's been a massive rise in lesbian groups being organised through websites like www.meetup.com and www.scenenomad.com. Anyone can set up an event and such websites have allowed women to take control in the face of exorbitant rents. 'Meetup.com is open to all sexualities so perhaps a little bit too open for those women who aren't out, whereas Scenenomad.com is specifically aimed at the gay market. If you're not "out", you don't necessarily want to join a gay group on Facebook because everyone in your network will see what you are up to. It's something event organisers don't always consider – these days most companies promote their events on Facebook and tend to rely on it but they forget that not everyone is "out" and on Facebook,' says Bennett.

Planet London is looking to organise more daytime events for lesbians in 2013, as their survey identified a real need for places to connect in a relaxed environment. The site is a fantastic resource for lesbians in the city and surrounding areas – the 'dating and making friends' section brings up all sorts of activities including a champagne dining and eating out club, a list of lesbian dating sites, Mint – a business networking site for gay women, Pink Date – speed dating, wine dating, mobile dating, and various online communities for women. Pink Lobster dating is a niche-dating site for femmes who like femmes – perhaps not so easy to identify, as many lesbians are socialising in mainstream venues. It has a launch event in February 2013 and features a blog and dating expert, which distinguishes it from other lesbian dating sites.

Check out Meetup and Scenenomad and see what you can find locally. My local LGBT community isn't really visible until you sign up to the mailing lists and see how much is going on. 'Once you start looking, there's loads to do,' says Bennett. I think this is true of dating generally – we moan about the lack of decent men and women out there but it's about getting into the right mindset and being present, seeing those opportunities day to day.

Bennett has also noticed a cultural shift and more LGBT events in the city: 'This year there have been four gay pantomimes in London,' she says.

Setting up an event

If you want to start up a new event the key thing is to market it properly. The Planet London ladies are happy to help women do this and have plenty of resources for best practice when using social networks such as Twitter. They suggest not relying on Facebook, as not all women are 'out' and on the site. Instead, use sites like www.meetup.com and www.scenenomad.com, and have your own website and mailing list. That way you can build up a customer base, which is something Facebook can't give you – you may have page 'likes' but you can't access email addresses.

You can host low-cost events at home, e.g. salons or hire a community or church hall for cheap. My local pub has a lesbian book club and a boudoir upstairs that I can hire to do Rude parties: informal get-togethers for women to buy sex toys and talk about sexuality. It's an opportunity to get a group of like-minded women together to talk about relevant issues, do a skill swap, and support a good cause.

Southbank Surfing, www.southbanksurfing.com, is a hugely popular social event in London, which shows there's a real hunger for friendly meet-ups that don't revolve around alcohol and loud music. It grew out of the Lesbian & Gay Film Festival and offers a space to 'surf sofas' and mingle with other gay women informally. There's no music or set-up, you just turn up and chat. After two years it outgrew Southbank and now has a new venue at The London Wall Bar & Kitchen. In the UK we have really embraced café culture so it makes sense to have more LGBT venues of this nature. We're also drinking less as a nation according to recent reports – the rising cost of alcohol perhaps – so it's making people a little more creative about how we date and network.

Mobile dating

There is a big interest in dating and communication apps and the market for lesbian dating apps has become quite competitive. In London, they are filling a need for connection given that the LGBT community is widespread and scattered across different zones. Savvy businesswomen are identifying ways for women to connect locally, in real time, using their smart phones. Most of us struggle to find the time to see friends and family regularly – let alone make time to date. We work long hours and don't always feel like travelling across town to have a drink.

Popular apps include DATTCH, Grindr, Brenda and WOW, and we'll see many more in 2013. So, how do they work? Turn your phone on, launch the app and it will tell you how many other (subscribed) women are in the local vicinity so you can say hello. Because there are less specific LGBT venues in central parts of town, many women are choosing to socialise in mainstream pubs and clubs, which make it harder to identify a potential date. This makes it a little bit easier as you can turn on the app and see there are six other lesbians in the venue. It's a fun and dynamic way of dating.

'There is a big interest in dating and communication apps and the market for lesbian dating apps has become quite competitive.'

Erotic boutiques

Many erotic boutiques are run by women and put on regular workshops, book signings and talks. Sh! Womenstore in London, Organic Pleasures in Edinburgh and She Said in Brighton are all run by women and have spin-off groups and events, such as Fannies Rule, a celebration of female sexuality run by Sarah Berry in London. She Said has recently relaunched and is planning a monthly women-only shopping night in 2013. Workshops cover the political and practical – from feminist porn discussion to sex tips, pleasure and how to use a strap on. I went to a book signing recently at She Said for After Pornified, Anne G Sabo's new book about feminist porn, which gave me an opportunity to network and find out more about female-friendly porn. It's an opportunity to meet other gay couples too.

A new trend in 2012 is the erotic book club – off the back of the *Fifty Shades* phenomenon. London has several including Velvet Tongue and the Mucky Book Club – run by sex writer Betty Herbert. It's a reading group for people who like saucy bits in their literature and features kinky crafts, live lit cabaret and more from a central London venue. If you like the idea, why not link up with your local library and set up your own?

Women's groups

Find local lesbian/bisexual support groups. A quick search online brings up a meetup.com group for lesbians who are separated and divorced, the London Bisexual Women's Group, and Kairos in Soho – all safe places where you can meet other women to talk about current issues – coming out, sexual health, family and relationships. They also offer an opportunity to mentor younger lesbians. You'll find similar groups listed via your local LGBT network. There are various projects on the go – my local library is running one to collate oral histories from LGBT community and wants volunteers to get involved by doing interviews.

Volunteering

Get involved in charities, LGBT or non-LGBT, in your area of interest – sexual heath, single parenting, kids in the community, drug or alcohol dependency. There are lots of festivals, including Gay Pride in various cities around UK, lesbian and gay film festivals. Contact your local university to see if they need help with research in women's studies/gender departments. Sussex University is currently doing research into alternative parenting and looking for feedback. Contact switchboards on national charities – do they have volunteer opportunities?

'I live near Manchester so attend Pride every year, which I love and thoroughly recommend being involved with.' (Kadie, 21).

'I am not heavily involved in the Leeds LGBT scene. I think I would like to be more though. I'm in the relevant Facebook groups so I do get updates. I think that I would rather get involved in supporting teen LGBTs with advice: I use Gayleeds.com and am also sorting out my workplace to get into the spirit of Leeds Pride. I think the main thing we have struggled with as a couple is finding support for people in the same situation as my GF [she has children from her

'Find local lesbian/bisexual support groups where you can meet other women to talk about current issues – coming out, sexual health, family and relationships.'

previous relationship and her partner doesn't]. I know of Pink Parents, but I am not willing to pay for advice when there must be other places providing it for free.' (JB, 37, Leeds).

'I was very involved in LGBTQ events at university and I was the LGBTQ equality officer for my college. I have attended and walked in Manchester Gay Pride parades fundraising for charities including the George House Trust (HIV and living in the North West). I go to Canal Street in Manchester a lot (aka The Gay Village) as there's lots going on there all year round.' (Robyn, 21, Manchester).

'A few years back I had a really bad relationship, which led to a breakdown and to me going out of my way to avoid anywhere where lesbians were. It's been odd not being involved in stuff, and my recent move to Hastings from Brighton is an attempt to rebuild this part of my life in a new, smaller place.' (Jo, 40, Hastings).

'The UK dating market is an easy way to dip your toe into the dating scene and a great way to expand your networks if you aren't based in the city. It also focuses your mind and forces you to think about what you are looking for.'

Online dating

The UK dating market is worth over £1m and most of the main players have a niche site for the LGBT community. It's an easy way to dip your toe into the dating scene and a great way to expand your networks if you aren't based in the city, or work long hours, single parent, etc. It is accessible and you can do coffee dates when you have the time. It also focuses your mind and forces you to think about what you are looking for – you will have to write a profile and answer some psychological testing questions on popular sites like eHarmony and Gay Parship. You can find sites for long-term relationships, casual sex, swinging or conducting an affair.

'Meeting someone online takes the hassle out of dating and allows you to concentrate on building a friendship or relationship over time; based on mutual interests and relaxed conversations that don't take place against a backdrop of loud music and copious amounts of alcohol,' say the team from Gay Parship.

I joined eHarmony recently and what I like about it is that you don't have to wade through online profiles that anyone can see (or have your own on public view). The site matches you to those you are compatible with after you've spent time filling in a questionnaire. Most people on there seem to be serious about finding a relationship because you do have to pay a monthly subscription. Even if there's no chemistry when you meet someone for coffee, chances are you will get on, and you'll make a new friend who lives locally.

It's also good for changing your mindset around dating and relationships as you can see there are lots of men and women out there looking for someone. It can help you move on from a previous relationship and recover some flirting and communication skills if you're a bit out of practice. Online messages are nice to receive and give you a bit of an ego boost. However, I would suggest limiting the time you are on there to focus your mind a bit. Set it to one or two months and use that time proactively to arrange dates – don't necessarily wait for people to approach you. Print off profiles and have a proper read through before you dismiss someone on the basis of how they look. It's easy to develop a 'sweetshop' mentality around dating online, i.e. there's plenty to choose from and this makes it easy to hit delete without having a proper read through profiles. Don't be too focused on finding 'a type' – is there someone who looks interesting and worth getting to know a bit better over coffee?

Writing a good profile

Sex and relationship psychotherapist Paula Hall has several tips on how to write a profile that will catch people's eye:

* Make it personal and as positive as you can – avoid clichés, be quirky and specific about likes and dislikes. This gives a better sense of your personality than a more general statement. Be detailed and use anecdotes to bring your profile to life. Write in the present tense and keep it succinct – don't ramble.

* Good pictures – a selection of you doing things you enjoy and make sure you are smiling!

* Watch your grammar and spelling – people have nothing much to go on so will notice the details. Get someone to proofread it for you if it's not your strong point.

* Ask a friend or family member how they would describe you if you are

'Don't be too focused on finding "a type" – is there someone who looks interesting and worth getting to know a bit better over coffee?'

struggling to list your best qualities – let's face it, we don't often sing our own praises. If you really hate the profile-writing business, Pen My Profile will do it for you – for a fee!

- Keep an open mind and don't be too prescriptive about your 'ideal' partner. Describe what qualities you want in a partner, rather than what you don't want!

Setting an intention

What are you looking for: a short-term fling, casual sex, sex partners, or a long-term relationship? Monogamous or open? Be honest with yourself and any partners you meet. Be as clear as possible – write an online profile or a mission statement, if you like. Visualise an ideal partner – what do you do together and how do they make you feel? What do you want to get out of this year in terms of relationships and friendships? Writer Alice Gorman wrote a 'magic list' – 100 qualities she wanted in a man and shortly afterwards, a man who matched her criteria strolled into her life (read her article in Oprah magazine, www.oprah.com/relationships/How-to-Find-Love-Do-Magic-Lists-Work).

'"Being happy within" is the main criteria for dating success.'

Mary Balfour, dating expert.

Changing your mindset

How open-minded are you to meeting new people? Do you chat to strangers and look around to see who's around you when you're out and about? Most of us are glued to phones and laptops so don't always see an opportunity or register someone's interest in us when it happens. It's about being present, open and relaxed. Make an effort to join new social groups, to look and feel good – invest in your appearance. Do things that you are passionate about and that give you energy, as this will bring you into contact with others who share your interests. Activities are great – anything that gets your heart racing and takes the edge off the formality of meeting new people. You will have something else to talk about and because you're doing something, it makes it easier to chat to several people during the day. Plan a couple of things like this to look forward to each month.

'Being happy within' is the main criteria for dating success says dating expert Mary Balfour (www.drawingdownthemoon.co.uk). She says she can always tell which women are going to be easy to find partners for – they are the ones at ease in themselves, relaxed and happy and 'not desperate' to find a man or woman. They aren't feeling a lack of or looking for someone to 'complete' or fix them in any way.

You can't love or desire someone else until you love and desire,' yourself so think about self-seduction – 'it starts with self-desire,' says Anna Samson. Raise your sexual energy by masturbating regularly – this opens up your energy and people can sense how centred you are. It sounds cheesy but you need to fall in love with yourself first, and celebrate all that you are and what you've achieved before anyone else can do that for you.

Creating a healthy partnership

Psychologist, lesbian dating and relationship coach, Dr Frankie Bashan (www.littlegaybook.com) expands on this idea: 'Even though we can't control where we meet our partner, there are many steps we can take to create a space that is stable, secure and ready for growth. This will increase your chances of meeting a happy, healthy partner. You may be asking, "how do I create that?" and the answer is by being open, secure in oneself, and taking risks to meet new people.'

Notice any negatives in your thought process, e.g. why you block yourself from doing things. 'I shouldn't spend money on online dating/new clothes/haircut' and take the opposite action. If you always wait for people to call you, call them. It all helps to open up your world instead of feeling that the walls are closing in. Practise saying 'yes' to all invitations you receive socially for a month and see what happens. Be open and receptive and go on lots of dates. Be present in your daily encounters and slow down – put the phone away in the café and look around and smile at people. Engage with people more generally – even if it's just the person on the checkout. As your energy opens and shifts, things will start to happen. Enjoy life more too rather than maintaining a mindset that it is a struggle.

'Practise saying "yes" to all invitations you receive socially for a month and see what happens. Be open and receptive and go on lots of dates.'

Bashan also recommends not being too exclusive, too early on in the dating game. 'You may be thinking that this advice is counterproductive, but becoming exclusive before you're in a committed relationship can be a mistake. Have you ever stopped accepting dates from other women once you've found someone you really like? Well, don't do it! Until you've clarified that you're in a committed relationship, keep your options open. This way you can maintain individuality and avoid making the person the centre of your world too early in the relationship. Ultimately, this can be a win-win situation, by dating other people you will just confirm how much you like that "one" individual more and it prevents you coming across as overly dependent.'

Summing Up

- 95% of the lesbian scene in London is centred around alcohol and loud music, making it difficult to have a proper chat and get to know women on a more relaxed level. There's a need for more daytime, informal events where you can have coffee and mingle. Networking via online sites like Meetup. com and Scenenomad.com are one way to find and set up new groups.

- Join your local LGBT community and get on mailing lists to find out what's going on. The scene is diverse but it won't bite you on the nose – you need to get out there and join in. Since starting to look I've found a gay choir, walking club, holidays and accommodation, speed dating, suppers, book clubs, and projects via my local library.

- Dating apps have taken the LGBT market by storm – they enable you to find out how many lesbians are in your local vicinity so you can break the ice and say hello. Check out DAATCH, WOW, Grindr and Brenda.

- Online dating is a convenient way to meet new women wherever you're based but be clear and focused when doing it. Join a reputable site that uses psychological profiling and charges a fee if you're looking for a long-term relationship. Think about what you are looking for and take time to write a personal profile. Use stories and anecdotes to bring it to life and make sure you include a few good pictures. Most of all enjoy the process and don't get too hung up on meeting a soulmate – go on several dates and keep an open mind.

- Follow your passions and get out there and do stuff that fires you up and makes you feel good – you will naturally attract people to you.

Chapter Six

Fantasy and Foreplay

Anne Seman, class instructor at Vulva University, believes we should expand our definition of sex to extend beyond intercourse. 'What we see, feel, taste and touch can all be part of our sexual experience. When we fantasise, read erotica, or pen erotic emails, we're experiencing a different type of sex. The lesson is about getting away from the genitals as a focus of pleasure and exploring the erotic potential of the rest of the body,' she says. The brain is our biggest sex organ, as Jack Morin explores in his book *The Erotic Mind*.

Psychologist Glenda Corwin expands on the idea of 24-hour foreplay in her book, *Sexual Intimacy for Women – A Guide for Same-Sex Couples*. In 1983, researchers Blumstein and Schwartz did a survey, which highlighted a subgroup of gay women who were still sexually active in long-term relationships. This 20% still had sex at least twice a month and were defined as SA – 'sexually active'. So, what's their secret? Corwin says, 'They understand the power and necessity of 24-hour foreplay. They purposefully and consciously recreate those conditions of limerance using intentional planning and behaviour. It's about planning time to connect with each other in a way that makes you want to be sexual.'

'The brain is our biggest sex organ.'

Developing your fantasies

'Fantasies are great ways to find out what you want sexually. You can try on new sexual activities, styles and genders in your fantasies. You don't have to be literal in interpreting your fantasy,' says Felice Newman, author of *The Whole Lesbian Sex Book*. 'That six-woman gang bang you revisit each night before sleep isn't proof of a death wish or a deep need to be defiled. It may be that you just want to give up control, have group sex, or be overwhelmed by your partner's desire for you.'

Top fantasies for women include:

- Anonymous sex/sex with a stranger

- Cross-orientation – fantasies of being a man or having sex with a man/group of men, and switching gender

- Dominating a partner – taking control sexually of the situation

- Submission and release – letting a partner take control of our desires

- Being disciplined for naughtiness

- Forbidden sex e.g. age-play – daddy/girl role play or daddy/boy

- Exhibitionism and 'being caught'

- Celebrity sex – having a famous partner

- Threesomes or moresomes/group sex

- Rape or forced sex 'against your will' with the woman as either the rapist/victim

'We've kinda done them all! We think of a fantasy and tend to let it happen in reality.' (DK, 45, Derbyshire).

'We don't share fantasies necessarily, but will try things out for each other. I'm more into BDSM than my partner is but she is trying different things because she knows I will like it. She has a thing about suits and suspenders so I wear those sometimes.' (Anon, 30, Midlands).

'I've always had a lot of sex! I've had a reasonably large number of partners over the years, always women, since I was 17. With my current wife we had a great deal of sex at first, several times a day, every day – but it does die down. Even now though (three years in the relationship, two years married) we go through spells of having sex every day, then life takes over and we're too tired to do anything but sleep. We use toys, especially vibes. In the past, I've had long-distance phone sex, which I loved, and experimented with most stuff at least a few times. In a previous long-term relationship (six years) we only had sex for the first two, which was frustrating; as once we hit a certain point it was impossible to contemplate ever doing anything rude with her again. This did eventually contribute to our break up.

'I find it odd that I don't think I've really done that [shared fantasies] with any partner – weird, maybe I need to think that through. In the past I've had a lot of phone sex which involves fantasies – it was great.' (Jo, 40, Hastings).

'My partner and I share some fantasies with each other and will play these out. At a play party in Vancouver I knew she had a fantasy around being fucked in the gents toilets as my 'boi'. I was happy to oblige. I have fantasies around being submissive but, in this relationship, it is more natural for me to be dominant. My partner knows about my submissive nature and we play it out by her biting and fucking me. She doesn't dominate me though. I express my submission more through my masturbatory fantasies. With my partner I am very happy to be more dominant.' (Anna, 39, Devon).

'We fantasise a lot, often my GF will tell me a 'story' while she fucks me, often about us being in public or a club for example, something we don't really want to do. Although we would like to go to a fetish club and watch other people fuck. We enjoy real lesbian porn together. We are both adventurous and we will do anything as long as it's consensual.' (Justine, 42, Middlesex).

Play parties

There are various sub-scenes of play parties (fetish clubs) to cater for different tastes and alternative lifestyles. Fetish clubs for gay women tend to focus around burlesque, drag and uniform – different ways to express your sexuality depending on what you're into. BDSM is also part of this scene, perhaps on a smaller level. Going to a fetish club with a partner is a chance to discover new things together, be inspired and turned on and develop trust and communication around sex – sometimes it's easier to talk about things when you can watch a play scene and engage with the women afterwards. Check out www.fetlife.com to see various clubs listed around the UK.

'There used to be a lot of fetish clubs in London (Klub Fukk, Hard On, Purrr, Pussy Control),' says Naomi Bennett of Planet London website. 'Many lost their venue and have closed. Corsets and Diamonds is popular burlesque [club] but lost its venue so is on hiatus. Club Subversion still runs but is irregular. Someone tried a strip night last year called SweetDreams but it didn't take off (it was pitched wrong and promoted to the wrong women). Wotever allows all kinds and many people dress up for that and the founder Ingo is a good person to talk to about the queer scene. They run a queer sauna every couple of months too.

'Rudegirlz started up recently – it has a bad website but seems to be going okay despite this. [The clubs are] all pretty public, use Facebook and it's not as underground so it seems like there is less stigma. Sh! Womenstore in Hoxton runs sex classes, but these are not lesbian only so they tend to be along the lines of 'how to give a good blow job'. Pace runs a sex and sexuality workshop.

'It is still quite a mixed, split scene. The queer end of the spectrum is more open-minded and will go to mixed events, play parties, etc. They have strict guidelines and rules that all adheres to respect. The more vanilla lesbians are those that prefer women-only venues, although some that know more gay men than women, or have been hurt prefer the gay Soho scene to lesbian events.' Bennett recommends checking out www.gingerbeer.co.uk to keep up to date.

In an article for DIVA magazine (April 2011) Mel Steel wrote about 'what happens inside lesbian sex clubs?' (www.divamag.co.uk). She reports on a new trend for lesbian sex clubs, which includes Lash For Lasses in Manchester; Klub Fukk, a polysexual, mixed venue; Steamy in Brighton and Purrr in London, a women-only fetish club. She points out that having sex in a public place is against the law in licensed premises (with the exception of private members' clubs). Women can be spanked or flogged or tied up to a cross but not have full sex (maybe the authorities turn a blind eye). 'What they offer is fetish-play in a sexy play space and a host of ways to indulge your imagination and creativity with like-minded women,' says Steel. She also interviewed Rosie Lugosi, organiser of Lash For Lasses (www.clublash.com) who says of the club:

'I'd say about 50% are hardcore BDSM dykes and about 50% are goths, performers, exhibitionists and people who just like dressing up. It's a very safe, inventive and creative space. We're open to all ages, sizes, body shapes, colours and abilities. We've had women come dressed up as evil rabbits and as fairies of the dawn! We gets lots of newbies, and make sure they get looked after by our dungeon mistresses.'

Hosting your own club night

If you have the space at home or can hire a venue locally why not set up your own club night? Mel Steel and DIVA have the following tips:

- Get the atmosphere right – use lighting and music.

- Make sure it's a clean and comfortable space.

- Have a dedicated area for people to get changed (Starkers, a naked nightclub for men and women in London had a black curtain, which didn't feel particularly glamorous or safe hence the club attracted mainly gay men). Women have accessories! Not necessarily the best for storing in a black bin liner!

- Have hostesses to show people around and explain the rules and equipment.

- Play etiquette – don't interrupt when other people are playing, don't touch other people's toys or equipment, don't try to play with someone else if you haven't been invited to, and don't let people play under the influence of drink or drugs. You can't consent if you're not sober.

- Organise a sexy performance, like a striptease.

- Play porn flicks or have some sexy magazines and pictures around the place.

- Make sure there's plenty of lube, condoms, gloves, etc.

- Have more experienced players there early to act as social butterflies and get the play started.

- Have some nibbles available for when the energy dips.

- Use the Internet (websites and message boards) to reassure nervous newcomers, get advice from more experienced players, or meet up to plan scenes or outfits in advance.

- After a party: check in with the person or people you've played with to make sure they're okay.

- Make sure everyone is over 16 years old

- Be creative, be safe and have fun.

Aural sex

I love dirty talk but I admit it's not always that easy to do, particularly when you've been together for a while. It's very powerful to hear the words 'what do you want?' to be told how desirable you are, and to hear a lover's breathing quicken after you whisper something in her ear. A friend who works as a pro-domme told me that she took vocal lessons to help express herself because she was shy in bed and it bothered her that she didn't make a lot of noise. She now has a trill whistle – various exotic bird-like noises coming out of her throat, which sounds very sexy. I also admire women who work on sex chat lines and are able to bring a man or woman to orgasm using their tone of voice and imagination. Call one up and learn a few tricks or two, and check out various books on the subject: Talking Sexy to the One You Love by Barbara Keesling, Carol Queen's Exhibitionism For the Shy, and Miranda Austin's Phone Sex.

Keesling suggests a simple exercise to help you let go, which is to talk dirty to yourself when you're masturbating. The idea is to let a stream of consciousness out and say whatever comes into your mind. Just keep talking and notice if it makes a difference to your orgasm. It does intensify things. Perhaps it's because opening your throat creates a better energy flow in the body. She believes being vocal is key to experiencing a full body orgasm.

The authors explain that we often find it hard to ask for what we want and that being a 'good girl' is something that is drummed into women from an early age. Other suggestions include recording yourself having an orgasm and sending it to your lover, and identifying words you find sexy and using them to tell your partner what you are doing to yourself, or want to do to her. Betty Herbert has written a funny book called The 52 Seductions and in it describes how she and her partner set about to seduce each other again for a year. One of their adventures was to call up a sex chat line together. She gave her husband a blow job while he chatted to the girl – probably the quickest phone call he's ever made. Why not have your lover wear a strap-on and try the same?

Lesbian porn

Lesbian sex is a popular genre in porn but most porn featuring 'lesbian' women is aimed at a male audience so it doesn't turn most women on. However, type 'real lesbian porn' or 'dyke porn' into Google and it's a different story. You'll find hot movies either directed by women or featuring real-life couples – bisexual and lesbian women, making the scenes hotter, intimate and more realistic than those fake plastic boobs, acrylic nails and fake orgasms found in mixed porn. There tends to be a whole body focus and emphasis on female sexual pleasure says Deborah Swedberg in NWSA journal (a feminist journal).

To find real lesbian porn – amateur and professional – do a Google search and check out some of the popular porn sites – Redtube, Kink.com. See Fatale Media, SIR videos, Pink & White Productions – Shine Louise Houston is described as the grand dame of lesbian porn, BLEU productions, and the CyberDyke Network. www.nofauxxx.com makes alternative porn for people of all genres and orientations. I've also come across www.hotmoviesforher.com and www.gooddykeporn.com.

There's been a rise in female porn directors too making quality videos – check out Candida Royalle, Zentropa's Puzzy Power, Anna Span, Jamye Waxman, Tristan Taormino, Libido Films, Petra Joy, Ms Naughty (aka Louise Lush), Erika Lust, and Jennifer Lyon Bell's Blue Artichoke Films. Read Anne G Sabo's book *After Pornified* for a full resource list.

Many lesbians also love gay man porn, according to online lesbian magazine *Lesbilicious*. 'It's real – you can't fake a hard-on,' commented one of their readers. They say: 'It may at first seem counter-intuitive, but the very fact that there are no women in gay man porn can remove a huge burden for some people'. It can be a turn off to see women in mainstream porn movies that clearly aren't enjoying themselves.

'Assuming we can safely discount penis envy as outdated Freudian twaddle, the answer to why lesbians enjoy gay man porn could partly lie in how we use porn as a way to play around with genders and sexualities outside of our usual experience. Watching gay man sex on a screen or a magazine is a peek into a forbidden world that we're usually excluded from. It's taboo and exciting, but at the same time totally fake and entirely safe.'

Whatever fantasy or fetish you can think of – there'll be some form of porn to cater for it. It's a chance to learn new tricks and be inspired for new ways to explore pleasure and fantasy alone and with a partner.

Lesbian erotica

Perhaps a little bit more portable, lesbian erotica will also inspire and turn you on. Most of the *Fifty Shades of Grey* sales were via Kindle and e-readers, giving women chance to read anonymously on public transport. There are 133 popular reads on 'Good Reads' at the time of writing including 'Best Lesbian Erotica'. Sh! Womenstore has a dedicated section of erotica for lesbians which features titles by popular authors in the genre – Janet Hardy, 21st century Kinky Crafts (how to make your own S/M toys), Susie Bright, Patrick Califa, Justine Elyot, Tristan Taormino, Susie Bright, Scarlett French, Alison Tyler, Rachel Kramer Bussel, Violet Blue, plus the infamous (now kinky) Black Lace titles. Popular anthologies include *Best Lesbian Erotica*, *Best Lesbian Bondage*, *Best Bisexual Women's Erotica* and *Best Butch Femme Erotica*. Classic novels exploring female sexuality can be found at Coco de Mer's London store: *Fanny Hill*, *Tipping the Velvet*, Anne Rice's trilogy, *Victorian Lesbian Erotica*. You'll also find books on dating, weddings, love stories, the Kama Sutra for lesbians, pregnancy, and a history of Sapphic love (The Erotic Print Society).

If you like writing and blogging and want to have a bash at writing your own, Black Lace run regular erotic writing seminars, and Eroticon is an annual conference for erotica readers and writers, based in London in 2013. Both will give you plenty of ideas, encouragement and new contacts to help you get started.

'Whatever fantasy or fetish you can think of – there'll be some form of porn to cater for it. It's a chance to learn new tricks and be inspired for new ways to explore pleasure and fantasy alone and with a partner.'

Summing Up

* It's important to fantasise regularly, read erotica, write erotica/emails/texts, and stimulate your brain and imagination to experience a different type of sex, says sex educator Anne Seman. Then we can explore the erotic potential of the rest of the body and it helps us to expand our definition of foreplay from something we 'do' to a partner before sex.

* Fantasies and fetish are great ways to find out what you want sexually and try new things. A trip to a fetish club will inspire you and build trust and communication with a partner.

* The play party scene for women is continually evolving – as club nights close new ones start up. Many things are organised online via Facebook, Meetup.com, Scenenomad.com and Fetlife.com, as well as ads in lesbian magazines DIVA and G3. Women's clubs offer a space for fetish play to stimulate imagination and creativity with like-minded women. Many are safe and welcoming to women who come alone too.

* 'Real lesbian porn' is a popular genre for women, as is gay man porn. Many female filmmakers are producing hot films that depict pleasure from a female perspective. Check out Anne G Sabo's book *After Pornified* for a list of producers and female-friendly erotic boutiques where you can find them.

Chapter Seven

Pleasure Toys

We've come a long way since the seedy backstreet sex shop of the eighties. *Sex and the City* introduced a new generation of women to the pleasures of the vibrator and made it more acceptable for women to talk about sex and buy toys. *Fifty Shades of Grey* did the same for bondage toys in 2012 – online boutique Lovehoney launched a range of toys to match the books for Christmas 2012 and the range has sold out. Many erotic boutiques (high street and online) are run by women and have a loyal customer base. 'Women like to shop with other women in environments that are sensual and comfortable, and lesbians are loyal to brands,' says Nic Ramsay, owner of She Said erotic boutique in Brighton. 'Lesbians don't like shopping with men around and they like the privacy and sensuality our boutique offers.' She is introducing a women's only shopping night once a month in 2013 and planning to host more salons on female pleasure.

Sex toy trends

'Sex is an active part of my life. I am happy with how often I have sex, but would also like to experiment more with toys and another female partner.' (Zoe, 20, Lincolnshire).

'The main trend is that sex toys are now used by all sexualities – they are versatile and not exclusive to heterosexuals or gays', say www.bondara.co.uk. For example, 'pegging' – the use of strap-on dildos and harnesses – is practised by both heterosexual and gay couples. The feedback I had from women that filled in my sex survey is that lesbians like to shop together, ask questions and try stuff on – it's difficult to buy a harness and strap-on over the Internet. Even dildos come in all shapes, sizes and materials so sometimes asking for advice in store is useful. Shopping together also opens communication around sex, you'll have a giggle and it breaks down inhibitions.

'Shopping together also opens communication around sex, you'll have a giggle and it breaks down inhibitions. It's good to talk about sex and pleasure in a neutral environment that is female-friendly and sensual.'

It's good to talk about sex and pleasure in a neutral environment that is female-friendly and sensual. You will see new things to test out, new books to read and feel informed and inspired by the conversations around you. Last time I visited She Said I came away with a sachet of ON Arousal Oil, a natural clitoral cream that is fantastic.

Part of the pleasure too is in touching toys and clothes – feeling them against our skin, noticing how they are to hold. Shopping for personal products like sex toys should be a visual, tactile and sensory experience – I find that more rewarding than shopping online but I see that has its benefits too – it's quick, easy and anonymous.

Toy materials

'Shopping for personal products like sex toys should be a visual, tactile and sensory experience.'

- Silicone – non-porous, smooth, firm and slippery feel, long-lasting. It's slightly more expensive but worth it. Easy to clean and retains heat to body temperature. You can't use them with silicone lube, however, as it will rot the toy.

- Latex – non-porous, cheaper and gets softer with use so will break down quicker. You can't use with oil-based lube as it destroys latex.

- Cyberskin – a newer material and very popular because it feels like real skin, a mix of silicone and PVC. It can be sticky and harder to clean.

- Jelly rubber/PVC – soft, quiet, comfy. Clean it with soap and water and avoid if you have sensitive skin – it has a strong smell!

- Glass/crystal – this looks and feels beautiful and tends to be used for smaller toys such as G-spot curved jade dildos. They have a firm texture and can be heated or cooled to suit so are great for G-spot or prostate play. They aren't so good for motion play, i.e. in a harness as they are quite rigid. Toys with ridges will have added sensation. Silicone lube works well with glass toys, as it is very slippery.

- Metal – very rigid like glass so is most often used for butt plugs and dildos – G-spot or prostate play. You can heat or cool it to suit.

Best-sellling toys for women

Here are the top selling toys in the lesbian/bisexual category, according to www.sextoys.co.uk:

- Anniix Fusion of Pleasure – invented by a lesbian

- Feeldoe Silicone Vibrating Double Dildo – the feedback I've had is that it can be difficult to use and slip out but is still a favourite and bestseller

- Loving Joy Double Pleaser Teaser

- Couples' Vibe – Screaming O Vibrating Tongue Ring

- Finger Vibes – Screaming O FingO Vibe

- G-spot Gel and Guide

- Creams – Tickle Her Pink and Nipple Teeze Gel

- Pumps – Advanced Vibrating Clit Pump

Sh! Womenstore also sells a lot of lube, leather 2-strap harnesses, and their Cupid's curved six-inch dildo.

However, the boutique owners I spoke to said they'd love to see more lesbian women and couples trying new toys and being more adventurous. It tends to be heterosexual couples adopting new trends first and having a go, for example, as with pegging. They will also buy new toys when they change partners. However, the process is different for gay women.

'The toys are an extension of themselves so the dildo they choose is very important. It's a process,' says Nic Ramsay. 'Gay women like to feel the toy, squeeze it and talk about it and they are prepared to spend more money on a good-quality toy. They sometimes share harnesses so can both take control with the strap-on. It's a good way to explore power play. Double-headed dildos tend to be bought by heterosexual couples having threesomes.' Feeldoe's double dildo has been quite popular but the feedback she's had is that it's quite tricky to use and can slip out.

Nic Ramsay has also noticed a trend away from lesbians buying phallic-shaped toys in the shop. 'Only 1 in 25 customers want a proper phallus,' she says. 'It's OK if the toy is mildly penile but generally gay women don't particularly want their dildos to look like a willy.'

So what does she rate and like? Israeli brand JOYA is high on her pleasure list. 'They are bullet-shaped toys, tapered and flare out at the end. The thin flap goes over the clitoris and you can wear it from inside like a harness. They give lots of clitoral stimulation and I think the toys are really well designed.'

How to choose sex toys

Anne Seman recommends figuring out what you want first of all and buying quality toys – go to the women-owned boutiques. Test out toys on yourself first before using them with a partner if you're not sure how the sensation will feel. It's also best to discuss using a new toy with a partner in advance – i.e. don't just spring it on her mid-play! Also decide:

* What kind of sensation and stimulation do you like? Where else on your body would you like to feel it? Clitoral, G-spot, breast, anal? Penetrative or non-penetrative?

* What do you have in your toy box and what's missing? Write a list of erotic things you'd like to try. If you like anal play, then try it with a glass, jade or metal toy. The sensation will be different particularly if you move around with the toy in place.

* Where do you like to play? Bath time privacy – look for waterproof toys. Cheeky play with your partner in a bar? How about a bullet or finger vibe that fits into your handbag or a remote control toy?

* Do you want to use toys together? Mutual masturbation toys include double-ended dildos such as the Feeldoe, and new fun board games such as TEASE.

* Noise factor – rechargeable toys such as LELO tend to be quieter to operate than battery vibes or plug-in ones.

* Kink play – BDSM toys come in range of prices and quality, from beginner lines such as Bondage Boutique from Lovehoney to seriously luxurious items on sale at Coco de Mer and Master's Desire. They open up the possibility of sensation and impact play and I'd recommend doing workshops first. You can learn how to use candle wax safely, spank a lover, and how to do erotic rope bondage.

- What intensity of sensation do you need to orgasm? Plug-in vibes such as Magic Wand are an essential staple and can deliver strong orgasm very quickly. You can also use them on your body for a general relaxing massage. If they are too strong reduce the intensity by putting a pair of silk knickers over the top.

- Where do you typically play? If it's confined to the bedroom how about some creative sex furniture such as Liberator wedges? These will open up play spaces and make oral sex more comfortable. A lot of sex furniture these days is discreet and you'd never know what it was by looking at it!

- Health issues – is mobility an issue? I've had bad knees this year with arthritis and found it difficult to be on top during sex so I used a wedge and cushion to make it more comfortable. Suspendible sex swings are great for this and can make strap-on sex more versatile and comfortable.

Book in a shopping trip and make a pact to try out a new toy each month. 'Just try sex toys, maybe you'll like them!' says Anne Seman. 'They're not just for couples that need help in the bedroom – marital aids. They remind us not to take sex too seriously.' She recommends the anthology *Toy Tales*, which explores fantasy and play through the use of toys and accessories.

'Sex is an active part of my relationship. Obviously in the beginning of our relationship it was a lot more frequent at several times a day. Now it's less frequent ranging from once a week to once a month. This doesn't bother me; we both have busy lives and work different hours and tiredness and kids get in the way. My partner has two children, both teens, from her previous marriage. I don't like having to be quiet during sex so we often wait 'til the kids are at their dad's for the weekend. We have a lot of variety in our sex life and use various toys: strap-ons and a little BDSM. We are very open with each other about what we want and like. Although the sex we have isn't in a major quantity anymore, the quality is fantastic and it's always mind-blowing.' (Anon, 30, Midlands).

'Lube is our number one sex toy. It transforms the way sex feels and makes it very sensual.'

Lubricant

Lube is our number one sex toy. It transforms the way sex feels and makes it very sensual. You can use it for all over body massage on your nipples, clitoris and internally for G-spot massage. It comes in a variety of textures and tastes for oral sex and falls into the following types:

- Waterproof – general purpose to use with condoms. Tends to dry out quickly so you can reapply or reactivate it with water. Compatible with sex toys, condoms and strap-ons.

- Silicone – great for anal play as it lasts a long time but not compatible with silicone toys and condoms. Not great for vaginal penetration as it's too sticky and hard to wash off.

- Oil-based – lasts longer but not compatible with latex condoms. My favourite is YES oil-based lube, which smells of chocolate.

There are lots of new natural brands on the market, which are female-friendly and won't upset vaginal pH or affect fertility (glycerine-free). Popular brands include YES organic, Maximus, PINK and LoveLube.

Dildos

These are non-vibrating toys used for vaginal penetration. You can attach them to a strap-on for pegging – anal or vaginal penetration. They are fun, popular and come in a range of materials, shapes and sizes, which will all feel different so it's best to go in store and have a look at them. Think about what size you'd like – medium-sized ones sell well and stimulate the G-spot and vagina comfortably. If you have had sex with a man and enjoy penetration go for a size that matches a penis size that felt good. If you plan to use them with a harness remember the harness takes up half an inch. Acrylic/glass dildos feel firm so go for a smaller size, as they will feel bigger. Curved dildos are great for G-spot or prostate play. You can also buy double ended ones for joint play, and ones that you strap to your chin for oral sex.

'It is very handy to have a variety of dildos when you are having sex, since each one can feel remarkably different,' says Mikaya Heart, author of *The Ultimate Guide to Orgasm for Women*.

Choosing a strap-on harness and dildo

Strap-ons are versatile and enable vaginal or anal penetration and cock sucking, and are often swapped between partners so both can explore sub/dom and gender play. They leave your hands free to explore other areas of the body. Harnesses come in different sizes and materials so if you're not sure which type to buy go shopping and try on a few. You need a good fit and a firm dildo so that it doesn't come out mid-thrust. The dildo is held in place by a rubber or metal ring so it can be adjusted if you change position.

Most are worn around the hips but you can also buy them for your thighs or chin. 'You may also buy harnesses that can be attached to different parts of the body, such as your thigh, so that she can sit on your knee or your chin, so that you can stimulate her orally while fucking her,' says Heart.

When it comes to penetration with a strap-on, it's a case of experimenting with different positions to see what gives you the most power or gravity. It is a very different feeling to fuck a woman with a strap-on rather than using your hand (fisting), says Heart. 'It's easiest to get a good effortless rhythm going if she is lying down and you are standing, perhaps at the end of the bed, or she may be bent over the arms of the sofa.' Experiment with height too – a step above or below her will alter the angle of penetration and stimulate different areas of the vagina. Heart also recommends sex slings, as they mean you can have sex standing up while your lady lies down.

'I think putting a dildo in a harness and strapping it to your body is so exhilarating. You feel so powerful, sexy and kind of like a big ol' freak,' says sex writer Jen Sincero. She recommends enjoying it as a recipient first and when you do take the active role, 'wear it well'. 'I highly recommend taking a little time to get used to your new member. Stroke it and play with it and imagine it can feel everything you are doing to it. Form a bond with it and try to make it a part of your body. Turn yourself on by jerking it off. Have your lover suck on it and stroke it. The more a part of you your strap-on feels like, the more connected to it you'll be when the time comes to penetrate your lover. This will make you more tuned in to what it's doing and how it's affecting her, making the experience hotter for both of you.'

An added bonus, she says, is that strap-on sex is a serious workout. You are using muscles you've never used before and it requires stamina and co-ordination. 'It was like learning to walk all over again – I had no idea how to access any of these muscles, and when I finally did it was a serious workout!' Take your time, find your groove and don't forget to use [put your body weight on] your arms if you can to make it feel more comfortable.

Vibrators

Vibrators come in all shapes and sizes for internal and external play. Finger vibes can be used for nipples, clitoris, perineum and anus. We have clit ticklers, Rabbits, G-spot vibes, anal vibes, waterproof vibes, tongue vibrators for oral sex, and harness-style vibes. Many are rechargeable and the plug-in styles (Hitachi Magic Wand) are extremely powerful – great for all-over body massage too. Generally, it's worth spending a bit more on a well-made vibrator as it will be made of body-friendly material (phthalate-free) and last a long time too.

Kegel vibes like Intensity and Pelvic8 are a bit of an innovation and do a dual job – tone up your pelvic muscles whilst giving you pleasure at the same time. Might as well make exercise pleasurable if you can!

'Generally, it's worth spending a bit more on a well-made vibrator as it will be made of body-friendly material (phthalate-free) and last a long time too.'

Anal toys

The anus is full of responsive nerve endings so using specially designed toys (with a flared base) can feel fantastic. If you pull a set of anal beads out when you orgasm it can intensify the sensation – giving you a 'fuller' feeling and a more powerful climax. Anal toys also stimulate the legs of the clitoris (crura) and G-spot because the wall between the rectum and vagina is so thin.

Inside the anus there are two sets of muscles (sphincters) – the first you can tense and relax voluntarily and the second automatically tenses when you try to insert a toy/finger/penis. So, pleasurable anal play is about taking your time, starting slow and using plenty of lube.

There are lots of anal toys on the market – beads, dildos and vibes. Here's a link to an article from Sh! Womenstore, which tells you how to make the most of anal play. www.sh-womenstore.com/faqdesk_index.php?faqPath=35

Breast play

Many women love breast play – nipples are often second in terms of sensitivity after the clitoris. Breast orgasms are quite common and it may be taboo, but many women enjoy breastfeeding for this reason. When you stimulate your breasts it releases oxytocin, a hormone that encourages bonding. It's not about breast size either – if you are small-breasted, nipple play can still be very erotic and pleasurable because the nerve tissue from nipple to breast is less stretched so there may be stronger sensation. The good news is the more you massage your breasts, the more responsive they will be (see Taoist breast massage techniques on page 49). Try massaging different areas of the breast – underneath, the nipple, areola and underarm, to see what is most pleasurable.

Various toys 'clamp' the nipple to create a pleasurable throb, particularly once you are aroused. Toys should be left on for no longer than 20 minutes as they restrict blood flow to the nipple. You will feel the most sensation/pleasure when you take the toy off or gently pull the chain (if wearing a collar attached to the clamps), as the blood flow rushes back to the area. Experiment, explore, and take it slowly!

Summing Up

- The main trend erotic boutiques have noticed is that sex toys are now used by all sexualities. They are versatile and not exclusive to heterosexuals or gays. Many couples use strap-ons (pegging) for vaginal and anal sex.

- Boutique owners would like to see more lesbian women and couples being adventurous in their choice of toys – perhaps trying new things in addition to a strap-on and harness. Gay couples are prepared to spend good money on quality toys and don't necessarily want to shop when men are around – something boutiques have picked up on. Expect to see more 'women only' shopping nights.

- Think about what type of sensation you enjoy and which parts of the body you'd like to pleasure before you go shopping. Are there things you haven't tried that you're curious about? Make a list of things you'd like to try. Test out new toys on yourself first so you know how best to use them and how they feel. Also, discuss any new purchases with a partner first rather than getting them out mid-play.

- Online boutiques are great – often cheaper than high street stores because they have less overheads but there's great value in a trip to a female-friendly boutique. They are sensual, tactile environments and you'll come away feeling inspired with new ideas for play. They also open up communication around sex if you go with a partner, which is never easy at the best of times – and best done outside of the bedroom.

Chapter Eight

Orgasm

I Love Female Orgasm by Dorian Solot and Marshall Miller is a refreshing new book on the subject – I like that it's gender inclusive and has a chapter called '*Coming With Pride*' – sex advice for lesbians and transgender/intersex folk.

We all love orgasms, and, most of us if we're honest, want sexual pleasure to end with one. However, it's important not to narrow down sex and intercourse to be about orgasm, says Mikaya Heart, author of *The Ultimate Guide to Orgasm for Women*. 'It's so much huger than that. Orgasm is one small aspect of this huge subject, but it is a very loaded aspect for most people and that tends to detract from the pleasure it might otherwise bring us.' Orgasm is also a personal thing and a learned response. We learn from a young age what feels good down there and how best to bring ourselves to climax quickly. And we tend to stick to these patterns as we get older – even though our sexual response and what we need to 'get off' may have changed.

It's very easy to get into a rut with masturbation and to get things over too quickly, which means we don't allow ourselves to stay on a sexual high for a long time – and therefore we don't know what is possible for our bodies. You need to be an intrepid explorer when it comes to orgasm and your own pleasure – practise regularly and try new things such as the practice of Orgasmic Meditation (OM) or 'OMing' – a term coined by Nicole Daedone to signal a mindfulness practice which is done in pairs and involves finger to genital contact. OM draws from Tantric practices, yoga and meditation as part of the 'slow sex' movement with the aim of bringing consciousness to sexuality to deepen your orgasms. Proponents describe it as more than orgasm, and say that it encourages greater emotional awareness, relationships and fulfillment. See www.onetaste.us to find a UK-based workshop.

Be prepared for the fact that orgasm can also be an emotional response and things can come up – tears, anger and frustration, which aren't always what we're expecting from sexual pleasure.

Try to widen your definition of orgasm and give yourself permission to stay fully aroused for a long time, says Heart. She explains that we are taught from an early age to control our bodies, bladder and anus through potty training and that control continues into adult life – if women have control issues and perfectionist tendencies they may find it hard to let go enough to experience orgasm fully. You can break this pattern through regular masturbation and giving yourself permission to experience pleasure over a set period of time rather than stopping after the first orgasm.

'Sex can evolve beyond orgasms. Sex can be transformed to become an individual vocabulary of erotic gestures, combining bodies to reach high states of arousal and desire, beyond a quest for orgasms by either woman or man. Sex can become something new, something we have not yet seen, something that we all now create by taking private, very courageous, steps,' says Shere Hite.

What is an orgasm?

On a physical level an orgasm is an accumulation of blood in the pelvic area and genitals through stimulation and fantasy, which reaches a peak and is then released causing the blood to flow backwards. This creates a feeling of expansion in the pelvis/whole body and orgasmic contractions at 0.8 seconds apart, according to Masters & Johnson's model of sexual response. Most female orgasms typically last around 15 seconds. As well as a deep physical release there's an emotional and spiritual release, a surrendering of mind and body and a sense of peace and fulfillment post-orgasm. They really can fuel your creativity and make you feel alive.

Woman to woman

The fabulous thing about being a woman, as Lou Paget, author of *Orgasm* explains, is that women can experience orgasm in up to 10 ways including mouth orgasm, breast orgasm, anal, and blended orgasm (clitoral and

'Most female orgasms typically last around 15 seconds. As well as a deep physical release there's an emotional and spiritual release, a surrendering of mind and body and a sense of peace and fulfillment post-orgasm. They really can fuel your creativity and make you feel alive.'

G-spot). Our sexual response is less linear and more circular than a man's, creating new possibilities for pleasure and we can have multiple orgasms within one play session – there's no refractory period so to speak. The benefit of having sex with a woman is that you already have a matching sexual response cycle so you will be naturally tuned in to each other's rhythms and nuances. There is no penetration anxiety, knowing that only around 30% of women orgasm from penetrative sex. With another woman you can take the time to really explore and get to know each other's bodies.

'I orgasm regularly, alone and with a partner. I have orgasmed with a woman and found it an easy and enjoyable experience. I find sex with both genders satisfying.' (Zoe, 20, Lincolnshire).

'I orgasm fine but I've not had an orgasm with a man. I would like to create an environment where I feel safe enough to try this!' (Cathie, 36, Lancashire).

'OMG. Sex with a woman is out of this world. My GF had several relationships before me so I guess you could say she has perfected her technique. My GF is my first lesbian relationship. When I kissed a girl many years ago, I should have realised then that I liked it! With a woman it is far more satisfying. People say that you are in tune with each other, which to a certain extent, yes, it's lovely. But sometimes when the rosy, lovey-dovey sex goes out of the window and it's just pure 'let's fuck' sex, it is amazing.' (JB, 37, Leeds).

'I do orgasm regularly. I've had sex with three men in the past and only one orgasm – during cunnilingus – with a man. I much prefer sex with women! I don't know if it's easier because I haven't evolved my sexuality with a man in the same way as I have with women. I've had several female partners and generally, very good sex, but it has depended as much on where I'm at with knowing my own sexual needs, desires, preferences, as it has on the fact that it's been with another woman.' (Anna, 39, Devon).

'I have found it far easier to have an orgasm with a woman, also the sex was more satisfying maybe because we enjoy each other more and took the time to really make sure we were both satisfied. With men it was always 'let's get it over with' – maybe that's just me.' (Lorraine, 45, Kent).

'I always orgasm with my GF and not only once, I can have three or four orgasms. When in heterosexual relationships I would hardly ever orgasm unless I was imagining I was being fucked by a woman in front of other women.'
(Justine, 42, Middlesex).

'Far far easier to orgasm more frequently and even at all compared to sex with a man. Sex is far more satisfying and exclusive with a woman because a) they know what they are doing, and b) I fancy them and not men!' (Kadie, 21).

'I always orgasm with my GF. In my opinion/experience orgasm is a lot easier with women than with men. I happen to find sex with men unsatisfying. I'm just not sexually attracted to the penis at all. I think sex is much more satisfying with a woman because women are beautiful, loving, sensual and more in touch with what they know feels good about the female body. Women can also be very naughty, daring and imaginative. I like how varied sex with women can be and the fact that there's an emotional connection as well as the physical attraction.' (Robyn, 21, Manchester).

'Orgasm is a complex process involving physical, psychological and emotional components.'

Orgasm and the brain

Scientific research into the effect of orgasm on the female brain is ongoing. Researchers at Rutgers University in the US are using brain imagery scanning techniques to find out what happens in the brain when we orgasm. Psychology professor Barry Komisaruk has found that almost every area of the brain is activated at orgasm, and the research aims to find out where the blockages occur in the 25% of women who don't, or rarely have, orgasms. We know that the parts of the brain governing fear and anxiety and inhibition close down when we orgasm – allowing us to fully express ourselves, relax and be in the moment. In that sense, orgasm is a spiritual experience when ego is out of the equation.

Researchers acknowledge that orgasm is a complex process involving physical, psychological and emotional components. Our understanding has moved on from Freud's thinking that clitoral orgasms were inferior to vaginal ones and we now know that the clitoris – the source of all orgasms – is much larger than we thought. Other sexuality researchers – Whipple et al have argued that more nerve pathways were involved than the pudendal (clitoral) – the parasympathetic nerve is linked to the G-spot, urethra and vagina.

What's clear, says Paget, is that orgasms are physical and mental, and blockages or orgasm problems often occur when we aren't at peace within or if there are communication and relationship issues or resentments. Orgasm is a living thing and your sexuality is continually evolving. Want to learn how to have a full body or multiple orgasms? There are some excellent books on the topic plus workshops online from orgasm experts like Betty Dodson. Also check out The New School of Erotic Touch website.

Exercise and orgasm

A first of its kind study by Indiana University researchers has confirmed anecdotal evidence that exercise can lead to female orgasm. They are often referred to in women's magazines as 'coregasms' because they are linked to abdominal work in gym. 'The most common exercises associated with exercise-induced orgasm were abdominal exercises, climbing ropes or poles, biking/spinning and weight lifting,' said Debbie Herbenick, co-director of the Center for Sexual Health Promotion at IU's School of Health, Physical Education and Recreation. 'These data are interesting because they suggest that orgasm is not necessarily a sexual event, and they may also teach us more about the bodily processes underlying women's experiences of orgasm.' Results are based on an online survey to 124 women who had exercise-induced orgasms and 246 women who had experienced sexual pleasure during exercise. About 30% of these women were not heterosexual. 'It may be that exercise – which is already known to have significant benefits to health and wellbeing – has the potential to enhance women's sexual lives as well,' says Herbenick.

The benefits of Kegel exercises

Which leads us nicely on to Kegel exercises. Regular PC exercises are probably the key factor in improving your orgasms. Aside from physical pleasure you won't be stressing about getting to the loo in time either, as they will stop light adult incontinence. They give you an ability to 'milk' a hand or strap-on and will increase sensitivity in the anus and perineum too. Marrena

Lindberg has written a book called *The Orgasmic Diet*, which combines dietary advice (fish oils, maca, dark chocolate) with PC exercises for stronger orgasms and explains that this 'accidental' diet has led her to become multiorgasmic.

How to do them

The PC muscle is a band of muscle or 'hammock' that runs from the front to the back of the pelvic area and holds your organs in place. Weight, age, gravity and childbirth all weaken it. The easiest way to identify the muscle is to stop/start the flow of urine. Once you've found it practise squeezing and letting go of the muscles during the day (not when you're peeing). Do 10 fast reps and 10 slower, and gradually build this up. As your PC muscles get stronger so will your orgasms.

There are also lots of good pelvic toners on the market and hybrid sex toys that give you clitoral stimulation at the same time as toning your muscles. Explore jade love eggs, Ben Wa balls, Smart balls (Lelo, Fun Factory, Teneo) – these you can wear during the day as you go about your business.

Ejaculation

Sexuality educator Deborah Sundahl has researched G-spot and ejaculation extensively for years and put together resources showing women how to ejaculate and what role it plays in female pleasure.

So, if you want to explore and have a go at ejaculating empty your bladder first as the pressure on the urethra can make you want to pee. Put a towel down on the bed. The G-spot may feel numb or painful if there is trauma to the area, scar tissue or a recent vaginal infection. Sensitivity is also affected by how turned on you are and where you are in your menstrual cycle (better to go exploring after a clitoral orgasm). Get into the right mindset too – really give yourself permission to open up your body and let go on a physical and mental level. Take some deep breaths before you begin to allow energy to circulate and move your pelvis around – don't get stuck in a fixed position.

Squat down on all fours and insert your index finger, pressing on the upper wall. The G-spot zone will feel slightly raised and bumpy. Try to visualise moving the tissue and give yourself a deep, internal massage. Experiment with strokes, press, hold and feel. Firm and constant pressure is best so G-spot toys can work well if your hand gets tired. After a while the area will feel warmer and softer – as if the vagina is really opening up. It can be quite an intense sensation – a full body orgasm – and distinct from a clitoral orgasm, which feels more localised and external. This is because two different nerve pathways are being stimulated.

Dorrie Lane, tutor at Vulva University says she finds clitoral stimulation the easiest way to have G-spot orgasm and ejaculate. 'As I begin to peak, I start to push out, and I squeeze, release, squeeze, push. (It's those PC exercises). Sometimes I fantasise that my clit is really big and the need to release is overpowering! Sometimes I fantasise my ejaculate is "healing water" and releasing it will make me feel better. The first time I consciously ejaculated, I felt as though I was peeing. Go with it, don't worry, everyone feels that way.'

Learning how to ejaculate is empowering and nurturing – I like her idea of 'healing water' and you can use it to 'let go' metaphorically at times of your life when you need to heal or let go of something – anger or emotion, or a past love – it's about not holding things in the body.

Types of orgasm

Multiple orgasm

Quite often a second orgasm can be more intense and give you an opportunity to experiment with ejaculation. Stop stimulating your clitoris after your first orgasm, breathe deeply and imagine energy circulating through your body, then go back to the clitoris but stimulate it in a different way to help build sexual energy again. Change your position – if you're on your back move to all fours and lean forwards. Move your pelvis around as much as possible and breathe deeply. Give yourself permission to come again. Post-orgasm lie on your side and let your body/mind integrate the experience. Visualise anything you want to bring about or imagine yourself letting go of unwanted emotions as you orgasm. This can be a very powerful exercise – a form of moving mediation that can help you shift blocks and emotions.

You can also try using G-spot toys such as the Lelo Gigi or Crystal Wand to stimulate your G-spot after a clitoral orgasm. Once you are turned on it will be much easier to pleasure your G-spot.

Extended orgasm

Here's a technique from author Mikaya Heart for a full body or tantric orgasm that enables you to ride a sexual peak for longer. 'You will be amazed at how long you can stay up there (in a state of ecstasy) when you give yourself permission,' she says.

'Try this one with a partner. You need to stimulate her clitoris to a peak before she comes then use your other hand to switch to her G-spot – giving her an internal massage using your hands or a vibrator. Alternate the two for a minute or so. The aim is to get her higher – peaking – but not orgasming and it requires concentration and discipline (you can tease her and tell her to ban orgasm, it's not allowed). Repeat this a few times and then tell her she can orgasm – this should give her a deep, prolonged orgasm and a sexual high that lasts for hours.

Playtime

Commit to an hour a week for self-pleasure and try to find different ways to give yourself an orgasm. Love and get to know your body – experiment with anal play if you've not tried it, use anal toys and a vibrator, try nipple clamps or pegs, bring in porn and fantasies and make some noise! The aim is to try and keep yourself 'up there' as Heart describes it, with high sexual energy so that you can experience extended pleasure and hopefully, a full body orgasm rather than stopping after one clitoral orgasm.

Touch yourself in different ways manually and with toys – when do you feel full, expansive, open and ecstatic? How do you like to be touched in different areas? Have fun with this – there are no expectations, it's simply an opportunity to get to know your body intimately in your own time and nurture yourself. Experiment with a full body orgasm by taking yourself to the edge (the point just before orgasm) stopping stimulation and then resuming it. 'Repeat this cycle seven times, or as near as you can manage,' says orgasm coach Dr Lisa

Turner, 'and you will then experience the excruciating pleasure of a full body orgasm,' which she describes as an endless wave of pleasure that fills your entire being.

Oral sex

'Licking, lapping, poking, sucking, swirling, kissing, rubbing, humming, and flicking – our mouths are incredibly sensual and versatile,' says sex writer Dr Pam Spurr. Most women love oral sex and find it the easiest way to orgasm. Tongues are precise, warm, wet and varied in their pleasuring – they can dip and dart inside the vagina to tease and gently nibble and suck a clitoris to orgasm. The underside of the tongue feels different to the top, and according to the Chinese ancients, who were well versed in female pleasure, there's a link between the tongue and the genitals. So, the giver gets as much pleasure from oral sex as the receiver. No wonder it's our favourite sex act.

Mikaya Heart describes the art of pleasuring a woman's vagina as like 'playing an instrument'. She suggests using your tongue 'anywhere on your lover's body: her face, ears and earlobes, neck, back, her feet and toes, hands and fingers, the insides of her elbows and knees, her underarms, her breasts and nipples, her wrists and ankles, her belly, the insides of her thighs and arms, as well as, of course, on her vulva'. Work your way slowly around her body to her mound of Venus and then press and hold it before you continue pleasuring. This allows a woman to relax completely – to be held and possessed by her lover.

'Use your lips to caress each labia in turn, taking the whole length of it into your mouth and sucking on it, perhaps nibbling gently with your teeth,' says Heart. She recommends taking your time and trying different movements, slow and fast – see how your partner responds and follow her body language. Use your fingers and toys internally if she likes it and maintain the same rhythm as that with your tongue. As she starts to peak keep doing what you are doing – slow and consistent. Now isn't the time to change technique!

Oral sex is not without anxiety though – we all worry how we smell down there, whether our lover is bored because we're taking 'too long to come', or whether the size and shape of our genitalia is normal, whatever that means (against porn standards). The book *Femalia* by Joani Blank challenges these preconceptions by featuring 32 full colour photographs of female genitalia. If your partner shares those anxieties tell her how beautiful she is and how much she turns you on. It's good for women to hear these things and it will help her to really open up, let go and enjoy her orgasms. It's impossible to open up and relax into full body orgasms, and ejaculation, if we don't feel comfortable, able to express ourselves and totally free with our lovers.

If you like giving her oral sex but hate the dreaded neck ache, try sex furniture – sex swings and Liberator wedges enable you to raise your lover's body to a level that feels comfortable for your neck and shoulders. Oral sex can take a long time so it's important to be comfortable before you begin. Experiment with positions too – she can drape her legs over your shoulders as you kneel between her thighs, or sit on your face so that you're 'forced' to give her pleasure, putting her in a position of power.

There are lots of great books on this topic – check out Violet Blue's *Ultimate Guide to Cunnilingus*, *She Comes First* by Ian Kerner, and *Sex For One – The Joy of Self-loving* by Betty Dodson.

Summing Up

- We tend to focus on orgasm as the end goal of sex but it's important to widen our definition of pleasure, as orgasm is so loaded. Many women love receiving full body massage as much as sex and orgasm. We tend to fall into patterns with masturbation and orgasm and it's important to learn new ways to give ourselves pleasure if we are to evolve with sex and spirit. Check out Betty Dodson's DVD series on her website www.dodsonandross.com to see different masturbation styles.

- Experiment with different types of orgasm – clitoral and G-spot, breast, fantasy and anal – use toys, breath and movement (Kundalini yoga is great for awakening sexual energy). Give yourself permission to stay up there with your sexual energy for a while after your first orgasm. Take a break and resume play and you may surprise yourself with the intensity of your next orgasm(s). Women have a much shorter refractory period than men and are capable of multiple orgasms.

- Strong PC muscles and a good diet (wholefoods, plenty of water, oily fish, dark/raw chocolate) will also improve the strength and duration of your orgasms, as well as giving you more energy for sex generally. Exercise regularly too to get the blood flowing through your body to your genitals.

Chapter Nine

Alternative Parenting

'We plan on being parents and married in the next 10 years. Being a lesbian doesn't mean I don't want life events that straight people have.' (Kadie, 21).

'We have talked about getting married and having children using a sperm donor, maybe in our late twenties'. (Robyn, 21, Manchester).

Fertility is big business – there are two annual conferences held in London: The Fertility Show and The Alternative Parenting Show. In 2012 The Fertility Show had over 3,000 visitors and 60 stands, with various seminars aimed at LGBT families. It is a commercial affair but very useful for research, says Kate Brian, journalist and author of *IVF – The Essential Guide*. 'It's a unique opportunity to get advice and ask questions – there are so many experts in their fields under one roof and you can speak to the clinics and get a feel for how they operate rather than relying on marketing materials. It depends on what you want. It does have its airy-fairy elements but you can take it or leave it. Have a look at the programme and see what interests you. People who want a baby can be vulnerable but that doesn't mean they lose their brain at the door!'

She also thinks it's a good thing that no press are allowed at the event, as it protects people and provides a degree of anonymity. 'When I was having my IVF treatment, I couldn't talk about it without bursting into tears. It's important to feel safe inside and to be open to talking to people, particularly as many lesbian couples may not have told people they are having difficulties conceiving or want a family at all. It's also very empowering to be amongst others who are going through the same issues as you.

'The most important thing is to be as informed as possible about fertility treatment options as it can feel overwhelming at times [with IVF]. It's drummed into us from school age that we must use contraception or risk unwanted pregnancy so it can be a shock when we don't get pregnant the moment we stop using it! There's a loss of control and women can feel that their bodies have let them down, they blame themselves – they aren't doing the right thing or eating the right foods. The more you know and understand about the process, the more you regain control over your life. The other thing that tends to happen is that people put their whole life on hold. They don't go on holiday or change jobs because they might be doing an IVF cycle so life reaches a standstill. It can be all-consuming so the more informed you are the easier it will be to make decisions.'

'I always have mixed feelings about The Fertility Show,' says Olivia Montuschi, founder of The Donor Conception Network (DCN). 'I hate the rampant commercialism of the (particularly foreign) clinics but it is a wonderful opportunity for people to get high-quality information and connections. DCN provides a haven from the high pressure selling, focusing as we do on social and emotional issues for families.'

'Changes in the law have led to a rise in the number of single women and lesbian couples seeking IVF via NHS and private means.'

The Human Fertilisation and Embryology Act 2008

This was an Act of Parliament to amend The Human Fertilisation and Embryology Act of 1990, and the Surrogacy Arrangements Act 1985. The changes allowed certain people, with relevant circumstances, to have more legal rights as the parent of a child. The amendment was mainly in response to technological developments, and changes in society.

One of the main differences was the replacement of the phrase 'the need for a father', which appeared in the 1990 Act, with 'the need for a supportive parent', in the evaluation of a future child's welfare following the use of fertility treatment, or a surrogacy agreement.

Changes in the law have led to a rise in the number of single women and lesbian couples seeking IVF via NHS and private means. In 2007 figures show 350 single women had IVF in the UK but by 2010 that had risen to 1,571. The number of lesbian couples given IVF doubled in the same period, from 178 to 417.

The main new elements of the Act affecting lesbians are:

- Requiring that clinics take account of 'the welfare of the child' when providing fertility treatment, and removing the previous requirement that they also take account of the child's 'need for a father'.

- Allowing for the recognition of both partners in a same-sex relationship as legal parents of children conceived through the use of donated sperm, eggs or embryos. Two mothers can now be registered on birth certificate as parents.

- Enabling people in same-sex relationships and unmarried couples to apply for an Order allowing for them to be treated as the parents of a child born using a surrogate.

Planning a family

If you've made the decision to try donor conception first there are some things you need to think about, says Olivia Montuschi from DCN:

- Where do you want to source donor sperm – friends/family, a sperm bank (anonymous donor) in the UK or overseas? Waiting lists are quite long in the UK and it can be expensive. UK rules on anonymity prevent many donors coming forward. Another option is to source an altruistic donor (no money involved) via ALTRUI – an organisation run by Alison Bagshawe (see the help list). She will explain how to find a local donor if you don't want to look abroad.

- When to talk to friends and family about it – what kind of reactions might you get? What are you going to say? How much information to divulge?

- Discussing your sexuality with your child when he/she is old enough.

- Knowing your child's rights. In the UK they can access information about the donor/father and make contact. Can they contact other families conceived by the same donor to find siblings? (Up to 10 donations permitted in UK law).

- Does the donor have any rights to know about the child or make contact if he wants to?

- Who will be the biological parent and how does the non-biological parent feel about this? How will she be kept involved in the process so she doesn't feel sidelined?

- Where can you get further support on donor children and the emotional impact – how they are thinking and feeling? Are there any alternative parenting studies so you can support them later on and discuss things?

Academic research

Susan Golombok is an academic who does research into lesbian families at the Centre For Family Research, Cambridge University. She says 'My research focuses on new family forms with an emphasis on parent-child relationships and children's social, emotional, gender and identity development in lesbian and gay families, single-parent families, and families with children conceived by assisted reproductive technologies including IVF, donor insemination, egg donation and surrogacy. Current projects include a longitudinal study of surrogacy, donor insemination and egg donation families from infancy to early adolescence, and a study of adoptive gay and lesbian families.'

'The problem with assisted conception,' says author Kate Brian, 'is that there is a lot of medical research [to help women] but little research into what happens after the birth – parenting doesn't end at pregnancy! What about the emotional and psychological implications of having a donor child?' Golombok did some research in this area and asked donor children if they wanted to contact their biological fathers. She found they did want to know, but were more interested in finding out about half-siblings (in the UK donor sperm can be used to father up to 10 offspring). If they had four or five siblings they wanted to meet them and build a relationship with them rather than with the father. They felt they already had parents so having a relationship with their biological father wasn't so much of an issue.

Telling the children

'The principles with regard to telling children about their conception with the help of a donor are the same for all family types,' says Olivia Montuschi from DCN. 'Basically the earlier you start, the easier it is. In fact, in lesbian and solo mum families children start noticing from around two that their family does not contain a father somewhere and they ask about it. Other children (not adults) will also ask. 'We don't have a dad in our family' is a response that will suffice until other children start to understand that it takes a contribution from both a male and a female to make a baby.

'Nothing changes with having gone abroad for donation. All children deserve to be told the truth about their conception and not being able to answer questions about the donor is not a reason for not telling. This was of course the situation prior to 2005 in this country. There are many donor conceived children/young people who are managing well without this information. The only difference now of course is that if parents choose to go abroad they may have to explain this choice to their child in the future, as there will be children conceived in the UK who can have information they cannot access.

'The key to combating negative attitudes, bullying, etc., is for children to feel proud of who they are and how they came into the world. This comes from having parents who are comfortable and confident with the choices they have made and who are able to communicate this attitude to children. In our Journal, there is a lesbian parent of two sons aged 6 and 8 who has never encountered a negative attitude. Her main issue is around having to "come out" all the time as a lesbian family and people being rather intrusively interested in it – not negative, just interested.'

L Group Families

Another organisation worth contacting is L Group Families (see the help list). They provide support and advice specifically for lesbians looking to start fertility treatment. See A Guide to Assist You to Become a Parent, written by a GP, IVF writer and their lesbian mums' group. They also run bi-monthly workshops for women who are having families this way, which cover the following topics:

* The law relating to lesbians having children

* Different options to conceive

* An overview of the many fertility clinics and hospitals and what to ask to make sure you get a good service and are able to make informed choices.

* Hearing from lesbian women about their journey to parenthood

- Support and social events for lesbians with children
- When trying for a baby has failed: what to do and how to cope
- Support while you are pregnant
- An overview of the support services available to lesbians wanting to have children
- Adoption as a lesbian

Their website is informative and has links to national news on LGBT parenting and the law.

Using donor sperm

'Using a sperm donor is a popular way for lesbians to get pregnant.'

Using a sperm donor is a popular way for lesbians to get pregnant (if fertility is OK). Typically, it can cost between £500-£1000. You can use sperm from a known donor or an anonymous donor via a sperm bank. You are given the opportunity to choose a local donor and you can select preferences – height, hair and eye colour. Various tests will follow – blood, urine and sperm tests and the insemination will take place via a licensed fertility clinic.

Pros of using a sperm bank are that donors have to give up parental rights (although your child can contact his/her biological father once he/she turns 18). Semen is also tested for diseases and health information collected to ensure the quality of the sperm. Cons include, sperm is frozen (which can affect its quality), it can be expensive (but not in comparison to other methods such as surrogacy/IVF), and you won't have an opportunity to build a relationship with the donor/father. Choosing a known donor gets around this problem and it's possible to find altruistic donors via ALTRUI (see the help list) who aren't paid for donating sperm. If you plan to use a known donor it's wise to have a parenting agreement to clarify costs, living, schooling (even though it isn't legally binding it is useful in the event of a dispute, says The Lesbian & Gay Foundation).

See the Donor Conception Network's website for advice and support. Contact details are in the help list.

Intra Vitro Fertilisation (IVF)

IVF involves taking eggs from the ovaries and fertilising them with sperm. The fertilised egg is then implanted back into the womb (typically the younger partner but it's possible for both women to be implanted if they are in good health) to give pregnancy a chance to start.

The National Institute For Clinical Excellence (NICE) makes the decision as to what treatments are available on the NHS. Current guidelines are that women aged between 23-29 can have up to three cycles of IVF on the NHS. This will vary by region so it's best to contact your local Primary Care Trust for information. It is partially funded by the NHS but you will have to pay for fertility drugs per treatment course.

Private treatment is another option if you don't meet the criteria for treatment on the NHS and will cost around £5,000 per cycle (some clinics do packages). 'We don't treat same-sex couples any differently,' says Julian Norman-Taylor, Consultant Gynaecologist at Chelsea and Westminster Hospital. He explains that there is a blood test available, which will give a good indication of the chances of success before you start treatment.

It can be a long, arduous process and there's no guarantee of a baby at the end of it. Current figures show that around 1 in 3 babies are conceived in this way, although new technologies are being developed all the time.

So, how can you improve the odds of it working for you?

'Get fit and healthy and stop smoking,' says Mr Norman-Taylor. 'That's the main thing and you can see a big difference in the quality of the eggs [of a non-smoking woman]. There's no point in eating organic carrots if you're still smoking. Also, you must take folic acid pre-treatment. Whilst being overweight isn't a drastic issue, it's a risk during pregnancy so it's best to get fit for pregnancy. Also, try to get any other medical conditions under control.'

'IVF involves taking eggs from the ovaries and fertilising them with sperm. The fertilised egg is then implanted back into the womb (typically the younger partner but it's possible for both women to be implanted if they are in good health) to give pregnancy a chance to start.'

Choosing a fertility clinic

See the Human Fertilisation and Embryology Authority (HFEA) website for guidance on choosing a clinic in the UK and overseas. www.hfea.gov.uk/. It regulates and licenses clinics in the UK and also has useful fact sheets on IVF techniques. Kate Brian has had two IVF children and explains the options in her book *IVF – The Essential Guide*. She says you need to consider various factors before choosing a clinic – location, culture, specialisms and waiting times.

'There isn't a right or wrong and it's not straightforward choosing a clinic. Look at their success rates. Can they offer you what you want? Do they have donor access to sperm? How long is their waiting list? Often success rates aren't vastly different in clinics so it's often about how you feel about the clinic – go to open days and talk to the staff. What kind of set-up do you feel comfortable with? Do you want a smaller, intimate clinic where the receptionist knows your name or a larger, slick clinic that feels more anonymous? It's a matter of choice.

'If you're thinking about using an overseas clinic bear in mind that assisted conception is tightly regulated here in the UK. All countries are different so it can be quite fraught working out the rules and regulations. When couples are going overseas to start a family they tend to do all the groundwork themselves. People are expected to absorb things very quickly and be up on latest medical research. These days couples know a lot about the medical science and are knowledgeable and hungry to find out more.'

Brian feels that in 2013 lesbian parenting isn't an issue compared to 15 years ago when she wrote her first book on IVF (1998). Then couples were more likely to face discrimination and attitudes. She spoke to one lesbian couple that found it challenging going through the system. They had to lie and the mother-to-be pretended she had a husband and they were subjected to extra assessments. Whereas attitudes were more supportive to single parents than lesbian or gay couples the situation has changed for the better.

Surrogacy

Surrogacy is an option for lesbian couples if IVF hasn't worked out or you prefer not to do it. Traditional surrogacy is when the eggs of a surrogate mother are inseminated by donor sperm (anonymous or known) and implanted back into her womb in the hope of pregnancy. Gestational surrogacy is when a donor egg is fertilised and implanted into her womb.

'Surrogacy is the process by which an arrangement is made with a carrying mother that she will hand over the child she gives birth to immediately after the birth and relinquish her parental status. This is an option for gay couples who wish to have a child together without sharing responsibility with the child's mother/s,' says Natalie Gamble, a fertility law specialist.

Surrogacy is legal in the UK but it can't be done on a commercial basis – i.e. you can't advertise for a surrogate mother. Going abroad does seem like an easier option (India being the top destination worldwide) but, says Gamble, 'It's important for lesbian couples to be aware that, whether they conceive at home or abroad, English law on parenthood still applies, which treats the surrogate mother as the legal mother of the child. If she's married, her husband becomes the legal father. If unmarried, the donor will usually be classed as the child's father.'

She explains that gay couples can apply to the court within six months of the child's birth for a 'Parental Order' to become his or her legal parent (whether or not they are in a civil partnership). The child will then be given a new birth certificate showing their status as legal parents.

Surrogacy is a complicated arrangement and there's no set 'cost' for it, says The Lesbian & Gay Foundation. 'Every surrogate mother decides how much to charge. In the UK, the mother's expenses would likely vary from £7,000 to £15,000. This would cover all expenses needed during the course of pregnancy e.g. maternity clothing, travel, etc. You would probably also have to pay for IVF treatment on top of that, usually to the tune of £3,000 per cycle.'

See www.surrogacy.org.uk and the help list for more information.

'Surrogacy is legal in the UK but it can't be done on a commercial basis – i.e. you can't advertise for a surrogate mother.'

Adoption and fostering

'My wife has a 20-year-old son, who has never lived with us but is part of our lives. I'd love a child, but it's just never been the right time and now my body has started menopause, so it's unlikely now. We are hoping to foster, which is really important to me. We have a civil partnership, which does make this relationship feel different to other long-term relationships I've had.' (Jo, 40, Hastings).

Adoption agencies deal with all types of couples – not just white, heterosexual married ones. Adopting a child gives you legal status as his/her parent (unlike fostering, which does not take away legal responsibility from the birth parents). The aim is to give a child support and a family home until he or she is an adult.

In November 2002, the Adoption and Children Act came into being, which allowed unmarried couples, including same-sex couples, to apply for joint adoption. The couple needs to be able to show authorities that they are in a committed relationship. Single lesbians can also adopt a child.

'You need to be over 21 to adopt in the UK, a UK citizen, and to have no convictions or police cautions for offences.'

You need to be over 21 to adopt in the UK, a UK citizen, and to have no convictions or police cautions for offences.

Adoption can be challenging, says the Lesbian & Gay Foundation: 'Many of these children will have experienced at the very least disrupted care through living with birth parents then foster carers. Many have experienced abuse, neglect, inconsistent parenting and may have witnessed levels of domestic violence, drug and alcohol abuse.' However, many adoptive parents say that it is also the most rewarding thing they have done – to give a child a new start in life and see him or her flourish and grow.

Overseas adoption

Statistics for overseas adoption are still relatively low in the UK compared to other countries – around 300 per year compared to 4,500 in Italy and 2,000 in Ireland. It's thought that this is because of a lack of awareness and information about the overseas adoption process and how it works. Cecile Trijssenaar is the founder of UK-based International Adoption Guide and is also an adoptive parent. Contact her to find out more about how the process works and how to get started. www.internationaladoptionguide.co.uk/.

Summing Up

- There are many options for gay couples looking to parent. The Fertility Show is a good starting point – it has an alternative parenting stream and seminars/workshops on various topics. You can talk to experts within a field and get a feel for the different fertility clinics – UK-based and overseas – if you're thinking of IVF treatment. However, go in prepared and keep your eyes open. Fertility is big business and of course clinics want your custom. Be as informed as possible about all the options – IVF, donor sperm, surrogacy, fostering and adoption.

- UK fertility practice and laws are tightly regulated, which does give couples some protection. The legal situation is less clear if you are looking overseas so weigh up the pros and cons.

- Have a Plan B – be prepared for things not going to plan and make sure your desire to have a family doesn't take over your whole life. It is one aspect of your life, so try to keep it in perspective.

- Useful organisations to contact include L Group Families and the Donor Conception Network. Both can tell you the options for parenting and things to consider before you start. L Group Families runs free workshops and a drop-in group for gay parents in central London. The HFEA regulates fertility clinics in the UK and can advise on success rates and newer types of fertility treatment. See the help list for contact details.

Chapter Ten

Civil Partnership and Marriage

What is the Civil Partnership Act?

Here's a brief history of the Civil Partnership Act, how it differs from marriage and the legislation currently in debate. We'll look at what it means in terms of your legal rights, and how to go about it (it's not as complicated as you may think!). This chapter provides a checklist of things to do (which you can download online from the Pink Weddings website, see the help list) and it will give you an idea of time frames.

The Civil Partnership Act 2004 was officially implemented on December 5th 2005. It was a big step forward for gay rights and take up was popular. Between the 5th and 21st December 2005 there were 1,901 civil partnerships in the UK and in the first year (2006) there were 18,059 civil partnerships (Office For National Statistics 2007). Gino and Mike Meriano, gay rights campaigners and founders of Pink Weddings, point out in their book *Civil Partnership – A Guide to the Perfect Day* (New Holland Publishers 2009) that they have seen a big change in the type of wedding since the start of the Act – 'a typical time frame [for planning] from 2005-2007 was 6-10 months. Since 2007-2008 we have seen more requests for lavish ceremonies, which take longer to plan'.

How does civil partnership differ from marriage?

'Civil partnership is a completely new legal relationship, exclusively for same-sex couples, distinct from marriage,' explains Meriano. 'The government has sought to give civil partners parity of treatment with spouses, as far as possible, in the rights and responsibilities that flow from forming a civil partnership. There are a number of small differences between civil partnership and marriage, for example, a civil partnership is formed when the second civil partner signs the relevant document, and a civil marriage is formed when the couple exchange spoken words. Opposite-sex couples can opt for a religious or civil marriage ceremony as they choose, whereas formation of a civil partnership will be an exclusively civil procedure.'

Who is it for?

'Basically it is for adult same-sex couples, who are not in an existing registered partnership, or married and are not closely related. Gay and lesbian couples can sign an official document at a registry office in front of the registrar and two witnesses. Registered couples will have new legal status as registered 'Civil Partners' and will be protected by a package of rights. This brings the UK alongside other European countries that recognise same-sex couples, including Canada, Belgium, Denmark, Finland, Germany, The Netherlands, Norway, Portugal, Spain and Sweden,' says Meriano.

To enter into civil partnership you need to be over 16 (or have a document signed by your parents or guardian if you are under 18) as well as a legal resident in the UK (see www.pinkweddings.biz for the lowdown on immigration rights if you or your intended are an overseas national). You must be free to marry and not related.

Why do it?

There are many reasons – as an expression and celebration of your love, to support women's rights and gay rights, to be part of history, for peace of mind and to safeguard each other and your family in the future. Cohabiting couples do not have the same legal rights as civil partners even if they have children together.

What are the new legal rights?

'Partners will access joint treatment for income-related benefits, joint state pension benefits, they will have the ability to gain responsibility for each other's children, and they will be recognised for immigration purposes and will be exempt from testifying against each other in court. In addition, if one partner dies the other will have the right to register their death and the right to claim a survivor pension. They will be eligible for bereavement benefits and compensation for fatal accidents or criminal injuries. Surviving partners will be recognised under inheritance and intestacy rules and will have tenancy succession rights. Civil partners will be able to accrue survivor pensions in public service schemes and contracted-out pension schemes from 1988. They will be treated in the same way as spouses for tax purposes,' says Meriano.

The Equality Act 2010

The Equality Act 2010 ensures LGBT people are treated in the same way as opposite sex couples by benefit agencies and councils. When it comes to your entitlement to benefits the assessment process is the same. Stonewall has produced a useful guide: *Civil Partnerships – everything you need to know* to provide an overview of the law. It contains information on immigration, benefits and tax, pensions, the importance of having a will, pre-nups, and how to dissolve a civil partnership. See the help list for their contact details.

What is the new Marriage (Same-Sex Couples) Bill?

This is a new piece of legislation being put forward in 2013 to enable same-sex marriages in England and Wales. MPs have already had a free vote and the majority opted to pass the Bill. The next stage will be discussion of the Bill in the House of Lords, and the Bill will be subject to greater scrutiny. Culture Secretary Maria Miller said recently on Radio 4's Today programme: 'We feel that marriage is a good thing and we should be supporting more couples to marry.' However, the Bill has divided Conservatives – over 200 are said to be against it as many feel it is constitutionally wrong (the Church of England's definition of marriage is 'the union of one man and one woman').

The new 'Marriage (Same-Sex Couples) Bill' will enable same-sex couples to marry in both civil and religious ceremonies, as long as the church has given consent. If you're already in a civil partnership then it means you will be able to convert this into marriage (e.g. have a second ceremony in an approved church).

Maria Miller is aware that not all religious institutions support the legislation and wants to offer protection for churches to 'opt out' if they wish. 'We are trying to make sure that there are protections here for churches who feel that this isn't appropriate for their particular beliefs.'

At the time of writing the Church of England and Roman Catholic religions oppose gay marriage and Quakers, Unitarians and Liberal Judaism are all in favour.

Getting started

There is a small amount of administration to register a civil partnership and once this is out of the way, the creative fun can begin. Go with your strengths and type of tasks you both enjoy – which of you enjoys admin and planning? Divide up tasks in the early stages and decide on key things – what type of ceremony do you want (small and intimate or large and lavish?), number of guests (over 50 and you may pay more in some hotels, for example). Download a checklist from Pink Weddings and decide who will do what. Block out time in your diary to work on the planning, so it doesn't get left to the end of the week when you are both tired. This ensures an equal division of labour and helps reduce stress and the feeling that one of you is doing more than your fair share. Also, rope in your friends and family. Give yourself a reward when you get something done to help you stay motivated.

The checklist

- Google 'Free wedding planner download' and you'll find several sites offering advice, resources and checklists/documents you can download for reference.

- Setting a date – what's your timeframe for planning? Typically it is around 1 year to 18 months from engagement although larger weddings may take longer. Many venues get booked up to two years in advance during the popular months. Once you've made a decision send out a 'save the date' card.

- Setting a budget and working out who will pay for what (family contributions, etc.)

- Invitations.

- Paperwork – stating your intention and paying the fees at your chosen venue.

- Ceremony and venue – what type of ceremony do you want and how big? Separate signing at a registry office and a ceremony elsewhere? The options are your local registry office, a registered religious building or a licensed venue such as a National Trust property, a private country house or hotel, which is useful if guests are travelling and need accommodation. Some hotels have packages for a set number of guests to stay over and have a 'wedding breakfast' on the day. See *Pink Weddings* or *Tickled Pink* online magazines for inspiration and resources. If you like a venue but want to keep looking you can provisionally book it for a set period of time.

- Evening entertainment – live music, toastmaster or alternative acts?

- Cars and transport.

- Food – an informal buffet or sit down meal? Wedding cake?

- Gifts – a wishlist or money towards your honeymoon/home?

- Speeches and readings – best man or woman?

- Choosing suppliers.

- Wedding dress or suit?

- Wedding rings?

- Honeymoon – whisk each other away straight after the ceremony or have several 'mini-moons' throughout the year.

The paperwork

You both need to give notice of your intention to enter into civil partnership at your nearest registry office (you both need to do this if you live in different towns, and you need to have lived in the area for at least 7 days). See the interactive search map on www.GOV.UK website to find your nearest registry office. There is then a 15-day waiting period before you can marry while the notice is publicised (names and occupation only) so that any objections can be lodged. Your application is then valid for one year.

Civil partnership ceremony

A basic registry office ceremony involves you and your partner signing a civil partnership document in front of a registrar and two witnesses. It can be as simple and cheap as this if you simply want to secure your legal rights. There is a £60 fee for couples to give notice of intention and a registration fee on top (around £40 for a registry office and more for a private venue such as a stately home, hotel or public space). The Civil Partnership Certificate costs £9.25 and can be ordered online via the General Registry Office.

You will need to take proof of your name, address and nationality and if you've been married before you need to take proof of your divorce or a death certificate for your former partner.

If you want more of a ceremony than this you can write your own vows and include music and readings (no religious vows or quotes) although there is no obligation to do so. You can also exchange rings – discuss your ideas with the registrar. You can keep your own surnames, one of you adopt the other or opt for a double-barreled surname – apply through Deed Poll website to do this as it's not automatic, see the help list.

Ceremonies can also take place in any licensed venue around the UK or overseas so you can have the signing and ceremony in a different location. See the Home Office website for a list of all approved civil partnership venues around the UK. The list includes castles, hunting lodges, spas and country hotels.

Role of a wedding planner

Hiring a wedding planner will take the stress out of the big decisions – using an established company such as Pink Weddings means you'll gain years of experience, contacts and tips from a couple that have organised many different types of ceremonies since 2005 (and their own as one of the first gay couples in the UK to have a civil partnership). They are useful for legal information, creative help and pricing and comparisons if you want a larger wedding and feel overwhelmed with the planning. They can help with catering, guest lists, setting (and sticking to) a budget – you'll have an idea of a benchmark against other similar weddings. They will give you personal guidance, anecdotes, confidence and support. If you both have demanding jobs with long hours, childcare and not much family involvement or support, it's worth considering. The fee you spend on a wedding planner may be negotiated and is likely to save you money in the long run, as they can get discounts on established suppliers, etc. Their role is to make sure you enjoy the day and don't spend all of it fretting over whether things are going to plan and making sure everyone is enjoying themselves.

You can also hire a wedding planner to help you arrange certain aspects of the wedding, e.g. the ceremony or music rather than the whole affair.

Useful resources

www.pinkweddings.biz

www.pink-wills.com

www.gayweddingsshow.co.uk

www.pinkweddingsmagazine.com

www.thepinkguide.co.uk

www.ukba.homeoffice.gov.uk (UK Border Agency advice on immigration rules and documentation)

Gino & Mike Meriano: *Civil Partnership – A Guide to the Perfect Day* (New Holland Publishers 2009)

Nicola Hill: *A Very Pink Wedding – A Gay Guide to Planning Your Perfect Day* (Collins 2007).

Summing up

▨ The Civil Partnership Act 2004 was implemented in 2005 and was a huge landmark for gay and lesbian couples. It is a new legal relationship, which gives same-sex couples the same legal rights as opposite sex couples. See Stonewall's guide to civil partnership, available to download on their website (see the help list).

▨ The type of wedding you can have is down to your imagination! It can be a simple signing in your local registry office with two witnesses (for a small fee) or you can incorporate non-religious readings, music, rings and walk down the aisle. You can also have the ceremony elsewhere – any venue in the UK or overseas that is licensed for weddings. Some approved religious venues are included in this – churches or chapels if you want a religious setting. Contact your local council to find your local registry offices and to see what else is on offer in terms of venues if you want to marry locally – it's down to budget really – you could wed in a castle in the Highlands if you wish!

▨ New legislation is being debated in parliament to enable same-sex couples to 'marry' in an approved church as well as having a civil partnership – two types of ceremony effectively. Couples that are already civil partners will be able to convert their partnership to marriage for a fee and have a second ceremony if they wish.

▨ Download an online checklist for wedding planning and check wedding websites, books and magazines for inspiration on the different types of ceremony. Talk to others and ask how they did it. Pink Weddings has recently launched a TV channel, a 'real life' gay wedding show for ideas and inspiration.

Help List

There are lots of sources of advice for lesbians and bisexual women. Resources include websites, magazines, chat forums, support groups, films, books, TV, charities and social groups. Your local LGBT group is a good starting point for information and will have a newsletter you can subscribe to for local listings. Libraries often have a LGBT reading section and links to book groups and related projects e.g. oral histories. It's helpful to have support and advice from people in a similar situation e.g. coming out, dating, parenting, single-parent holidays.

Charities/helplines

FFLAG (Families and Friends of Lesbians and Gays)

FFLAG, PO Box 495, Little Stoke, Bristol BS34 9AP
Tel: 0845 652 0311
www.fflag.org.uk
Support and advice for family and friends of lesbians and gays.

KENRIC

BM K, London, WC1N 3XX
Tel: 07788 164731
www.kenric.org
Kenric is the longest established national organisation offering a social network to lesbians throughout the United Kingdom. Eclectic, diverse, discreet!

Lesbian & Gay Foundation

5 Richmond Street, Manchester M1 3HF
Tel: 0845 330 3030
www.lgf.org.uk
Registered charity fighting for and supporting LGBT people.

London Lesbian & Gay Switchboard (LLGS)

Helpline: 0300 330 0630

www.llgs.org.uk

London Lesbian & Gay Switchboard (LLGS) provides an information support and referral service for lesbians, gay men, bisexual, trans people, and anyone who needs to consider issues around their sexuality. All volunteers identify as lesbian, gay or bisexual. 24-hour support for issues around love, sex and life.

Pink Therapy

www.pinktherapy.co.uk

BCM 5159, London WC1N 3XX

Tel: 0207 836 6647

Email: admin@pinktherapy.com

The UK's largest independent therapy organisation working with gender and sexual diversity clients.

The Safe Network

NSPCC National Training Centre, 3 Gilmour Close, Beaumont Leys, Leicester LE4 1EZ

Tel: 0116 234 7217

www.safenetwork.org.uk

Support for groups in their efforts to help parents and families understand, accept and support their LGBT children. Support for bullying in schools.

Stonewall

Tower Building, York Road, London SE1 7NX

Tel: 0800 050 2020

www.stonewall.org.uk

National charity working for equality and justice for lesbians, gays and bisexuals.

The Turing Network

www.turingnetwork.org.uk

Community-driven directory for LGBT life with links to over 3,000 resources.

Coming Out support

The following books are recommended by Pink Therapy (you can buy through the website, www.pinktherapy.co.uk):
Together: A Guide to Love, Life and Lube by Patrick Gayle, Gay Times Books, 2001.
Coming Out Every Day by Brett K Johnson, New Harbinger Publications, 1997.
The Other Side of the Closet: The Coming Out Crisis For Straight Spouses and Families by Pierce Buxton, New York John Wiley & Sons, 1991.
Outing Yourself: How to Come Out as Lesbian or Gay to Your Family, Friends and Co-workers by M Signorile, New York Random House, 1995.

Dating & relationships websites

www.compatiblepartners.net (eHarmony's LGBT website)
https://uk.gay-parship.com/
www.planetsappho.com
www.gaydargirls.com
https://soulmates.guardian.co.uk/lesbian
www.thepinksofa.co.uk
www.pinklobsterdating.co.uk - for lipstick lesbians, launched in February 2013.

Female-friendly erotic boutiques

Female-run boutiques selling quality sex toys, female-directed porn, erotica and sex guides, fetish clothing, massage and sensual accessories. They run classes and workshops in female sexuality, and feature online blogs and sex news and features.

Coco de Mer
Tel: 0800 011 6895
www.coco-de-mer.com

Jo Divine
Tel: 01892 888 284

www.jodivine.com

Masters Desire

Luxury leather bondage gear and restraints handmade in the UK
www.mastersdesire.com

Sh! Womenstore

57 Hoxton Square, London N1 6HD
Tel: 0207 613 5458
www.sh-womenstore.com

She Said Boutique

11 Ship Street Gardens, The Lanes, Brighton BA1 1AJ
Tel: 01273 777 811
www.shesaidboutique.com

Lesbian and gay magazines

DIVA Mag

Millivres Prowler Ltd, Unit M, Spectrum House, 32-34 Gordon House Road, London NW5 1LP
Tel: 0844 856 0637
www.divamag.co.uk
Europe's leading lesbian magazine. Features UK news, lifestyle, dating, entertainment, sex, health and shopping. Has a chat forum called The Blue Room.

G3 mag for lesbians/Bisexual women

Square Peg Media Ltd, 37 Ivor Place, London NW1 6EA

www.g3mag.co.uk

Founded in March 2001 by Sarah Garrett, now available online to download. Features celebrity interviews, features, previews, reviews and listings, travel, music and film, arts, bars and clubs, leisure, community, fashion, health and fitness, property and sales, plus a new legal section.

On Our Backs (back issues)

The first women-run erotica magazine, and the first to feature lesbian erotica for a lesbian audience in the US. Published in 1984 by Deborah Sundahl and Myrna Elana. In 1996 a photography book called Nothing But the Girl was published (Cassell Press), based on the work on the magazine's artists. A complete set of On Our Backs is available from Brown's University library for review. See Susie Bright's blog (former editor) for details, http://susiebright. blogs.com/History_of_OOB.pdf.

Lesbian and gay websites

Bisexual.org

www.bisexual.org/US-based site providing worldwide resources for information on bisexuality.

Gingerbeer

www.gingerbeer.co.uk

Gingerbeer.co.uk is the local area information guide for the lesbian and bisexual women's community. Find special events and listings for bars, clubs, community groups, social groups and professional services. Originally created to cover the London area, coverage is now national. The site is primarily for lesbians and bisexual women but open to all those who have an affinity with the community. With free listings and free access, Gingerbeer.co.uk is a comprehensive guide for those providing resources, as well as those who want those resources.

Lesbian.com

www.lesbian.com

Relaunched in May 2012, Lesbian.com aims to create a hub for lesbian life globally and empower women and lesbians all over the world.

Lesbian.org

www.lesbian.org

Lesbian.org first began in the mid-1990s and was one of the first major websites for lesbians. For many years the site provided a comprehensive list of web links and also hosted discussion lists and websites for lesbian-oriented non-profits. The site also sponsored a lesbian literary journal called Sapphic Ink. Now undergoing a revamp, opportunities available for scholars and non-academics to write columns.

Planet London

www.planet-london.com

Planet London is a listings and lifestyle website that makes it easy for all lesbian, bisexual and queer women to find out and share what's on in London. Whatever your tastes, whatever you're into, whatever you want to know; what club nights are currently running, finding a local group to join, where to meet other lesbians or where's a good place to go on a date; you'll find it on the Planet London listings pages.

Marriage and Civil Partnership

www.civilpartnershipinfo.co.uk

Free guide for gay and lesbian couples in the UK considering civil partnership.

Deed Poll

www.deedpoll.org.uk

Information and advice about officially changing your legal name.

www.en.wikipedia.org/wiki/civil-partnership-in-the-united-

kingdom

All about civil partnerships in the UK.

www.gayweddingshow.co.uk

Annual gay and lesbian weddings show – dates for conferences around the UK.

www.pinkweddings.biz

Website run by gay rights campaigners and wedding planners, Gino and Mike Meriano. Help with organising your day, sourcing suppliers and a celebrant. They also publish *Pink Weddings Magazine*, and can provide comprehensive information on your legal rights.

www.pink-wills.com

Consultations at your home or your place of work specialising in will writing and personal estate management for gay couples either cohabiting or civil partners and singles. Inheritance tax, property protection, Enduring Power of Attorney, Children's Trusts, Disabled Child Discretionary Trusts, storage of essential documents and more – run by Susan Elkington.

www.pinkweddingsmagazine.com

New gay magazine for those wanting to plan a civil partnership. Showcases innovative and exciting ideas for your ceremony, reviews the latest trends from suppliers and venues, and gives advice on suggested etiquette and legal requirements that are now in place, both in the UK and abroad.

Parenting

The Alternative Parenting Show

www.alternativeparenting.co.uk

The Alternative Parenting Show is the original and biggest show of its kind. It provides a one-stop shop, which gives valuable information to same-sex and heterosexual couples and single men and women on how to make the dream of having a family a reality.

ALTRUI

www.altrui.co.uk
Egg donation service, for women who would like to donate eggs and those who need an egg donor in the UK.

The British Association of Adoption and Fostering

www.baaf.org.uk
Saffron House, 6-10 Kirby Street, London EC1N 8TS
Tel: 020 7421 2600
mail@baaf.org.uk
The UK's leading adoption and fostering membership association. The website is packed with useful information.

Centre For Family Research

www.cfr.cam.ac.uk
The Centre for Family Research is a multidisciplinary research institute within the Department of Psychology at the University of Cambridge. It has an international reputation for its research on families, and attracts visiting scholars from all over the world. The Director of the Centre is Professor Susan Golombok.

COTS (Childlessness Overcome Through Surrogacy)

www.surrogacy.org.uk
Moss Bank, Manse Road, Lairg IV27
Tel: 0844 414 0181
info@surrogacy.org.uk
Information and advice for those who are thinking of having children by surrogacy, or of becoming surrogates. An associated group called Triangle puts intended parents in touch with surrogates.

The Donor Conception Network (DCN)

www.dcnetwork.org
A supportive network of 1,600 mainly UK-based families with children conceived with donated sperm, eggs or embryos, those considering or undergoing donor conception procedures; and donor conceived people. If you or members of your family are affected by any of these issues, you have come

to the right place. Welcomes couples and individuals – heterosexual, lesbian, gay, single, married, divorced or cohabiting – who are facing issues about donor conception at any stage, and would like to hear the experiences of those of us who have been there before. Also welcomes professionals working in this area and donor conceived adults.

The Fertility Show

www.fertilityshow.co.uk
With a programme of 60 talks and 100 exhibitors, from clinics to nutritionists, The Fertility Show is the place to get answers. 3,200 people discovered this in 2012.
2-3 November 2013 Olympia, London.

Insemination Help

www.insemination-help.com
insemhelp@aol.co.uk
Advice on artificial insemination at home with an online shop for equipment to make the process as simple and effective as possible.

L Group Families

Tel: 07738 240625
www.lgroupfamilies.org.uk
Supporting lesbians by providing specialised information and advice on different services in the UK so you can make an informed decision about parenting. Has a booklet on 'alternative parenting' options, £5, and runs drop-in groups in London and free workshops.

Surrogacy UK

www.surrogacyuk.org
Voicemail: 0845 5577319
samesexcouples@surrogacyuk.org.
Excellent online advice about surrogacy plus social events at which potential surrogates and intended parents can meet.

Self-pleasure advice and instruction

Solo Touch

www.solotouch.com
Forums about masturbation techniques, and erotic stories.

Vulva University

www.houseochicks.com
Provides e-courses.

Alt Sex Stories Text Repository

www.asstr.org
Home to over 1,000 authors of erotic literature, host of the alt.sex.stories.
moderated newsgroup, mcstories.com, mirror site for nifty.org, and host of
several popular erotic literature archives.

The-Clitoris.com

www.the-clitoris.com
Provides all the information you need to know about the clitoris.

Betty Dodson With Carlin Ross

www.dodsonandross.com
Intelligent articles, tutorials, and DVDs from the 'orgasm doctor'.

RPM (The Rejuvenating Power of Masturbation)

www.therpom.com
Hosted by Dr William 'Bila' Kolbe. Historical, cultural, spiritual, and medical
dimensions of masturbation based on 30 years of research.

Sexual health

Services at GUM (genitourinary medicine) clinics are free in the UK: STI testing, advice on contraception and pregnancy, and sexual assault referral services. You can make an appointment or use a drop-in service. Find your local clinic via the NHS: http://www.nhs.uk/servicedirectories/Pages/ServiceSearchAdditional.aspx?ServiceType=SexualHealthService
See also: NHS Live Well advice for LGBT people: www.nhs.uk/livewell/LGBhealth/pages/lesbianhealth.aspx

Birmingham Wellbeing Centre for LGBT

www.blgbt.org
New forward thinking Health and Wellbeing centre in the city's Southside district, designed to meet the needs of the LGBT community. Opened to the public on 29th January 2013, the centre is the first of its kind to open in England and Wales and will strive to address health inequalities witing the community.

FPA

www.fpa.org.uk/helpandadvice/findaclinic
Aims to help establish a society in which everyone has positive, informed and non-judgemental attitudes to sex and relationships; where everyone can make informed choices about sex, relationships and reproduction so that they can enjoy sexual health free from prejudice or harm.

Need - 2 - Know

Available Titles Include ...

Allergies A Parent's Guide
ISBN 978-1-86144-064-8 £8.99

Autism A Parent's Guide
ISBN 978-1-86144-069-3 £8.99

Blood Pressure The Essential Guide
ISBN 978-1-86144-067-9 £8.99

Dyslexia and Other Learning Difficulties
A Parent's Guide ISBN 978-1-86144-042-6 £8.99

Bullying A Parent's Guide
ISBN 978-1-86144-044-0 £8.99

Epilepsy The Essential Guide
ISBN 978-1-86144-063-1 £8.99

Your First Pregnancy The Essential Guide
ISBN 978-1-86144-066-2 £8.99

Gap Years The Essential Guide
ISBN 978-1-86144-079-2 £8.99

Secondary School A Parent's Guide
ISBN 978-1-86144-093-8 £9.99

Primary School A Parent's Guide
ISBN 978-1-86144-088-4 £9.99

Applying to University The Essential Guide
ISBN 978-1-86144-052-5 £8.99

ADHD The Essential Guide
ISBN 978-1-86144-060-0 £8.99

Student Cookbook – Healthy Eating The Essential Guide
ISBN 978-1-86144-069-3 £8.99

Multiple Sclerosis The Essential Guide
ISBN 978-1-86144-086-0 £8.99

Coeliac Disease The Essential Guide
ISBN 978-1-86144-087-7 £9.99

Special Educational Needs A Parent's Guide
ISBN 978-1-86144-116-4 £9.99

The Pill An Essential Guide
ISBN 978-1-86144-058-7 £8.99

University A Survival Guide
ISBN 978-1-86144-072-3 £8.99

View the full range at **www.need2knowbooks.co.uk**.
To order our titles call **01733 898103**, email **sales@
n2kbooks.com** or visit the website. Selected ebooks
available online.

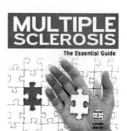

Need - 2 - Know, Remus House, Coltsfoot Drive, Peterborough, PE2 9BF